"A resonating strength of [this] book is the attention to detail…descriptions for accessing the trailheads, for following the trails, for potential problems along the way are presented with such clarity almost anyone can follow them.

We are dealing here with a man who loves the outdoors, and obviously loves sharing it with others. I'd highly recommend any Schad book on these subjects."

—TOM CUSHMAN,
former *San Diego Union-Tribune* sports editor and columnist

**ORAFA Publishing Company, Inc.**
**1314 South King Street, Suite 1064**
**Honolulu, Hawaii 96814**

Please send me the following *HOW TO GET LOST AND FOUND* books. I understand that I must send cash, check or money order with this order.

Name_____

Address_____

City/State_____ Zip_____

Shipping Address *(See Below)*

| TITLE | PRICE | P&H | QNTY | AMOUNT | Shipping Address ** GIFTS |
|-------|-------|-----|------|--------|---------------------------|
| AUSTRALIA | 9.95 | | | | 1 2 3 |
| CALIFORNIA | 9.95 | | | | 1 2 3 |
| COOK ISLANDS | 9.95 | | | | 1 2 3 |
| FIJI | 9.95 | | | | 1 2 3 |
| OUR HAWAII | 9.95 | | | | 1 2 3 |
| JAPAN | 9.95 | | | | 1 2 3 |
| NEW ZEALAND | 9.95 | | | | 1 2 3 |
| TAHITI | 9.95 | | | | 1 2 3 |

Hawaii Resident add 4% Sales Tax

Outside USA, add $1.50 per book for additional P&H

TOTAL

***Postage and Handling:***
*Book Rate:* Add $2.00 for first book and $1.00 for each additional book. (Allow 4-6 weeks.)
*Air Mail:* $3.00 per book
***For gift shipments:*** Specify address below and circle appropriate number on the order form above in the last column next to the title to be shipped. Items **not** so marked will be shipped to your address.

1st Address_____ 2nd Address_____ 3rd Address_____

_____   _____   _____

_____   _____   _____

A GIFT FROM:_____

Message will appear on label

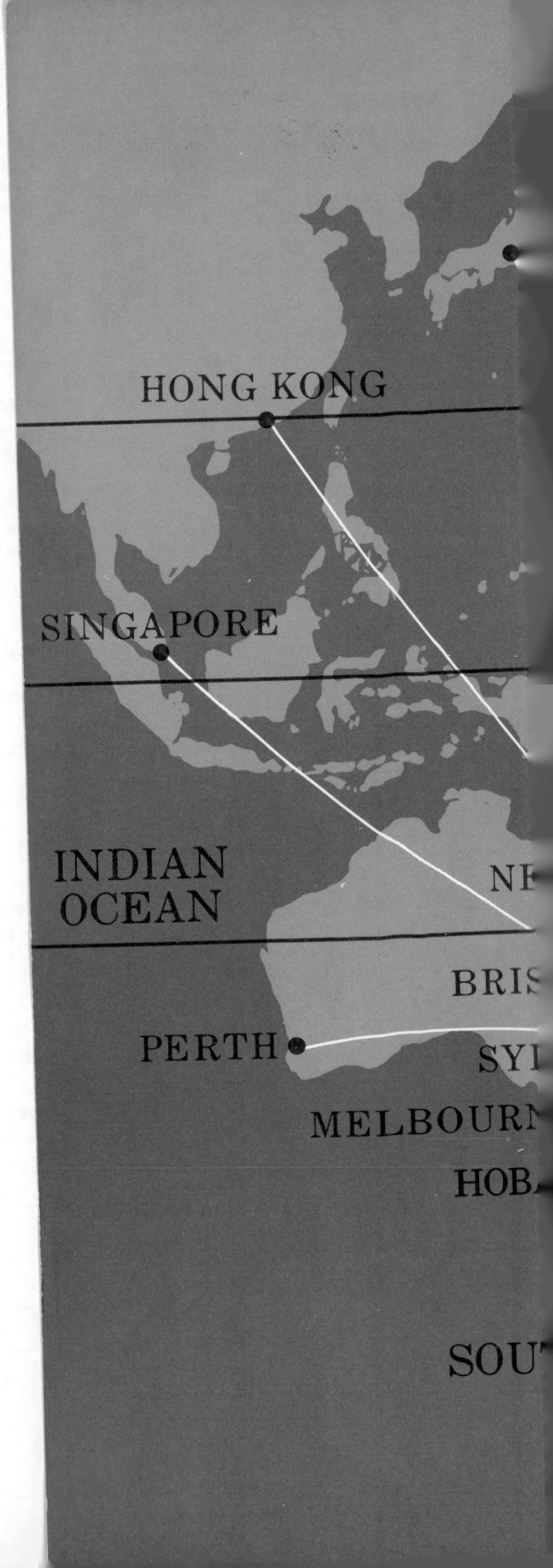
HONG KONG
SINGAPORE
INDIAN
OCEAN
PERTH
MELBOURN
HOB
BRIS
SY
NE
SOU

**ORAFA Publishing Company, Inc.**
**1314 South King Street, Suite 1064**
**Honolulu, Hawaii 96814**

Please send me the following *HOW TO GET LOST AND FOUND* books. I understand that I must send cash, check or money order with this order.

Name_____

Address_____

City/State_____ Zip_____

Shipping Address *(See Below)*

| TITLE | PRICE | P&H | QNTY | AMOUNT | Shipping Address ** GIFTS |
|-------|-------|-----|------|--------|-------|
| AUSTRALIA | 9.95 | | | | 1 2 3 |
| CALIFORNIA | 9.95 | | | | 1 2 3 |
| COOK ISLANDS | 9.95 | | | | 1 2 3 |
| FIJI | 9.95 | | | | 1 2 3 |
| OUR HAWAII | 9.95 | | | | 1 2 3 |
| JAPAN | 9.95 | | | | 1 2 3 |
| NEW ZEALAND | 9.95 | | | | 1 2 3 |
| TAHITI | 9.95 | | | | 1 2 3 |

Hawaii Resident add 4% Sales Tax
Outside USA, add $1.50 per book for additional P&H

TOTAL

*\*Postage and Handling:*
*Book Rate:* Add $2.00 for first book and $1.00 for each additional book. (Allow 4-6 weeks.)
*Air Mail:* $3.00 per book
*\*\*For gift shipments:* Specify address below and circle appropriate number on the order form above in the last column next to the title to be shipped. Items *not* so marked will be shipped to your address.

1st Address_____ 2nd Address_____ 3rd Address_____

_____   _____   _____

_____   _____   _____

A GIFT FROM:_____
Message will appear on label

Running along La Jolla Shores

50 Great City and Country Runs

# TRAIL RUNNER'S GUIDE

## San Diego

Jerry Schad

 WILDERNESS PRESS · BERKELEY, CA

**Trail Runner's Guide San Diego**

First EDITION January 2004
   2nd printing March 2006
   3rd printing 2009

Copyright © 2004 by Jerry Schad
Front cover photo © 2004 by Jerry Schad
Back cover photo © 2004 by Jerry Schad
Interior photos by Jerry Schad
Maps: Jerry Schad and Fineline Maps
Cover design: Courtnay Perry
Book design: Courtnay Perry

ISBN 978-0-89997-308-1

Manufactured in the United States of America

Published by: **Wilderness Press**
             **1345 8th Street**
             **Berkeley, CA 94710**
             **800-443-7227; FAX 510-558-1696**
             **www.wildernesspress.com**

Visit our website for a complete listing of our books and for ordering
information.

Cover photos: Running at Fish Creek (front);
             Sea dahlias, Torrey Pines (back)
Frontispiece: Beach Run

**SAFETY NOTICE:** Although Wilderness Press and the author have made
every attempt to ensure that the information in this book is accurate at press
time, they are not responsible for any loss, damage, injury, or inconvenience that
may occur to anyone while using this book. You are responsible for your own
safety and health. The fact that a trail is described in this book does not mean
that it will be safe for you. Be aware that trail conditions can change from day
to day. Always check local conditions and know your own limitations.

# ACKNOWLEDGEMENTS

Several people, directly or indirectly, have contributed to the creation of this book. In Tony Sucec's jogging class at SDSU some 30 years ago, I learned some crucial lessons about exercise physiology and the importance of good running footwear. That's when I caught the trail-running bug—and I haven't stopped since.

Over the years I've shared many running adventures in wild spaces with Don Krupp, Nick Soroka, Carl Johnson, Don Endicott, and Barbara Amato.

Sincere appreciation goes to Tom Winnett, founder and publisher emeritus of Wilderness Press. Our association of nearly two decades has resulted in several Wilderness Press titles written by me.

Thanks also to Jannie Dresser and Mike Jones, who moved this project along in the early stages, and to Roslyn Bullas, who kept the momentum going. Jessica Lage and Elaine Merrill ably edited this book, and Courtnay Perry masterminded the interior and cover design. Bart Wright of Fineline Maps designed the trail maps.

*Jerry Schad*
La Mesa, California
November 2003

# TABLE OF CONTENTS

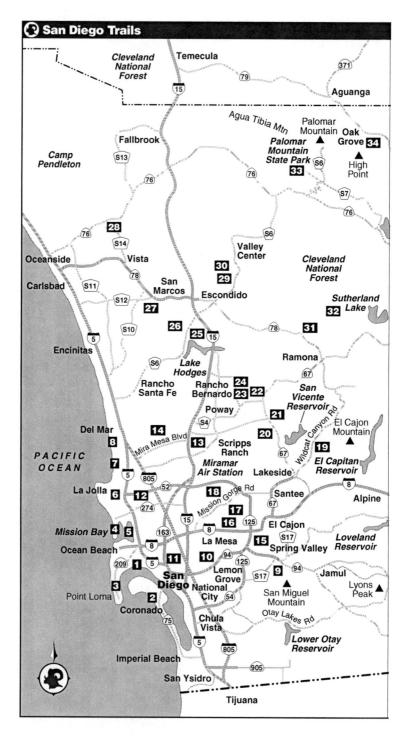

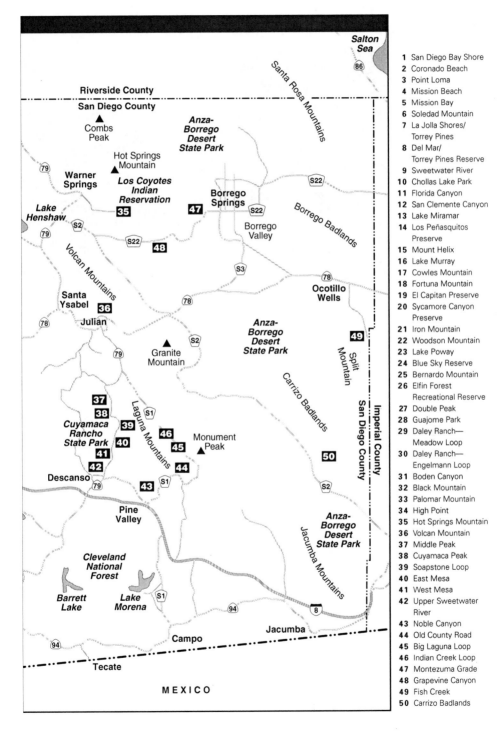

1 San Diego Bay Shore
2 Coronado Beach
3 Point Loma
4 Mission Beach
5 Mission Bay
6 Soledad Mountain
7 La Jolla Shores/
   Torrey Pines
8 Del Mar/
   Torrey Pines Reserve
9 Sweetwater River
10 Chollas Lake Park
11 Florida Canyon
12 San Clemente Canyon
13 Lake Miramar
14 Los Peñasquitos
   Preserve
15 Mount Helix
16 Lake Murray
17 Cowles Mountain
18 Fortuna Mountain
19 El Capitan Preserve
20 Sycamore Canyon
   Preserve
21 Iron Mountain
22 Woodson Mountain
23 Lake Poway
24 Blue Sky Reserve
25 Bernardo Mountain
26 Elfin Forest
   Recreational Reserve
27 Double Peak
28 Guajome Park
29 Daley Ranch—
   Meadow Loop
30 Daley Ranch—
   Engelmann Loop
31 Boden Canyon
32 Black Mountain
33 Palomar Mountain
34 High Point
35 Hot Springs Mountain
36 Volcan Mountain
37 Middle Peak
38 Cuyamaca Peak
39 Soapstone Loop
40 East Mesa
41 West Mesa
42 Upper Sweetwater
   River
43 Noble Canyon
44 Old County Road
45 Big Laguna Loop
46 Indian Creek Loop
47 Montezuma Grade
48 Grapevine Canyon
49 Fish Creek
50 Carrizo Badlands

# INTRODUCTION

Call it trail running. Call it mountain running. Call it adventure running. Or even survival running. Whatever label we attach to it, this increasingly popular modern sport existed long before the advent of Adidas or Nike footwear.

For many millennia, humans all over the world have run long distances, often over rugged terrain, for a variety of reasons. In Ancient Greece, for example, the legendary messenger Pheidippides is celebrated for his last act, a 25-mile dash from the battlefield at the Plain of Marathon to Athens to bring news of the Persian defeat. That deed, of course, is celebrated in the modern marathon foot race, which actually covers 26.2 miles.

The pre-Columbian Incan empire in South America maintained an orderly existence by an intricate system of roads stretching hundreds of miles, and by a communications network that utilized relay-running messengers called chasquis. The chasquis were stationed in huts at intervals of 2 to 4 miles apart. Messages, transmitted by spoken words or encoded in knotted, multicolored cords, were passed from one runner to the next, and could move as fast as 200 miles a day.

Running was a part of the hunting rituals of some Native American cultures. In communal antelope and rabbit drives, for example, Native Americans in the Southwestern U.S. herded their prey into V-shaped corrals or netted traps. Until about a century ago, the Tarahumara Indians of Mexico's Chihuahua state hunted deer by patiently tracking them at jogging pace until the hapless animals dropped from sheer exhaustion. The Tarahumara also have a long history of jogging 50 or 100 miles up and down the steep trails of Barranca del Cobre (Copper Canyon) simply for ritual entertainment.

Over time, the need to run for practical reasons evolved into running and walking for sport. One to two hundred years ago on both sides of the Atlantic Ocean, there was considerable popular interest

Opposite page: Chimney Creek, Palomar Mountain State Park

1

in a sport called pedestrianism. This is akin to what many runners today know as ultra-running, or ultramarathon running. Pedestrianism began strictly as a practice of walking exceptionally long distances, but it soon evolved into "go-as-you-please," a mixture of walking and running. A renowned British pedestrian by the name of Captain Robert Barclay capped his career with a walk of 1000 miles in 1000 hours. The American Edward Payson Weston attracted considerable attention in the second half of the nineteenth century for numerous long-distance walks or go-as-you-please journeys between disparate points on the North American continent. Perhaps his crowning achievement was a 77-day journey from Santa Monica to New York City in 1910. Weston was 72 years of age at the time.

During the 1920s, the Boston Marathon, already in existence for a quarter century, began to attract national attention. Ultra-marathoning entered a new realm with the staging of a transcontinental footrace by promoter C.C. Pyle. Nicknamed the Bunion Derby, it was to cover 3400 miles of the nation's fledgling highway system, from Los Angeles to New York, in the spring of 1928. Runners were to pass through hundreds of cities and towns, generating publicity, spectators, and hopefully money. Alas, expected funds from chambers of commerce never materialized. Runners were poorly fed and sheltered. Newspaper accounts ridiculed the race, calling it an "aching dog sideshow," a "tin-horn sideshow," and the "flop of the century." On day 84 the winner, Andrew Payne, crossed the finish line and graciously accepted first prize (a worthless $25,000 check), then staggered into a concrete pillar and fell unconscious.

With the coming of the Depression and World War II, interest in distance running and other sports inevitably declined. Then, with the return of prosperity in the postwar years, running again began to capture the imagination of the public. The sport grew slowly until about the 1970s, when it exploded in popularity. Much of the increased interest was due to an enhanced awareness of the benefits of vigorous exercise. With the environmental movement kicking in at about the same time, many runners turned their attention toward trail running. Running was becoming a way of exploring nature by touring on two feet, just faster than hiking.

Today, runners who tire of pointless circuits on the track or on city sidewalks look for and find aesthetically pleasing landscapes— trails in parks and natural areas, inside or outside the cities. Those who thrive on competition, but also like to hit the trails, have plenty of choices these days. Hundreds of competitive events featuring trail running take place annually in the United States. The San Diego region alone hosts more than 20 of them. Trail-running enthusiasts span a gamut between casual weekend warriors and dedicated athletes whose lives center around a circuit of races with lengths of up to 100 miles.

All of this brings us to the subject matter of this guidebook, which is written for residents of San Diego County (3 million strong) and the millions more who visit the region every year. Herein we proffer 50 running routes through the county's scenic coastal, foothill, mountain, and desert landscapes. You don't have to be a fanatical runner to enjoy them. None of the routes are longer than about 16 miles, and few involve elevation changes of more than 2000 feet. They are a starting point for exploring the region in running shoes.

Next time you feel like going out for a run in our neck of the woods, think about substituting trails for sidewalks, beaches for boardwalks, and fire roads for the automobile-dominated city streets. Introduce an element of opportunity and adventure into your workouts. Go where the wind takes you!

## WHY RUN HERE?

If there's a paradise on Earth for runners, it can be found right here in San Diego County. The region's coastal climate is nearly as benign as possible—and in certain seasons, our eastern mountains and desert can be just as agreeable. About one third of San Diego County (which is roughly the size of Connecticut) consists of lands in the public domain, open to recreation. Anza-Borrego Desert State Park and Cleveland National Forest in the inland area account for most of this land, while dozens of smaller state parks, county parks, and wildlife preserves comprise the rest. Urban and suburban development continues to spread over the coastal hills and valleys—yet at the same time much private land is being deeded over to public agencies for open-space parks and recreational trails. Ironically, as the total acreage of natural landscape in the county slowly declines, more miles of trail are becoming available for self-propelled travelers in the remaining open spaces.

Sea dahlias in
bloom at Torrey
Pines State
Reserve (Run 3)

Athletic enterprises—plus a healthy appreciation of our beautiful
city and backcountry—are the norm for San Diegans, not the exception. San Diego is nationally recognized for its sports-oriented and
health-conscious population. Sports such as hiking, running, mountain biking, and triathlons are booming here. You will be in good
company when you hit the trails.

## GETTING AND STAYING IN SHAPE

Anyone capable of running continuously for an hour on flat ground
has already had the basic training necessary for nearly all of the runs
in this book. To get to that basic level—if you are not yet there—
you'll need to devote, ideally, several hours a week to vigorous exercise. You can begin by walking at a fast pace for a half hour or a full
hour, several times a week. As the weeks go by, mix in increasing
amounts of running so that it eventually becomes the major part of
each workout. If you visit a gym, you can substitute certain forms of
exercise that involve the leg muscles, but keep in mind that even
though bicycling and the use of cycling machines improve your car-
diovascular fitness, you'll still need to work the specific muscles that
walking and running employ.

Exercise can be divided into two categories: aerobic and anaerobic. In aerobic ("with oxygen") exercise, the lungs and circulatory
system deliver an adequate supply of oxygen to sustain muscle
energy over a long period of time. In the more intense anaerobic

("without oxygen") exercise, the demand for oxygen exceeds the supply coming in. You're soon gasping for breath, your heart races, and you inevitably move toward exhaustion. A rather long recovery time of reduced effort or rest is required to reverse the condition of "oxygen debt" that accompanies anaerobic exercise.

It's a misconception that trail runners should emphasize anaerobic exercise. While it is true that short intervals of anaerobic exercise are highly beneficial for trained athletes, finding comfort at a reasonable pace is of prime importance for the trail runner. You are training to tour, not to sprint.

Once you have attained a basic level of fitness—the ability to run on easy terrain comfortably and continuously for a least 30 minutes—you can start hitting the easier trails in this book, most of which are "city" routes. With a more robust preparation of running continuously for an hour on easy terrain, you'll be ready to try out some of the more challenging "country" routes in this book.

On those more challenging routes, you will be forced to develop new mental and physical skills. On rutted, rocky, or slippery trails, you can't be sure that your foot will land on stable, flat ground. Instead, each foot plant becomes tentative. You must constantly observe and make quick judgments: shorten or lengthen your stride, step right or left, raise your foot to clear or push off of a rock or exposed root, lower your foot to step into a depression. Gone, perhaps, are rhythmic arm swings. Your arms become useful as counterweights to correct minor imbalances or to regain your equilibrium after a misstep. You'll learn to think ahead, making judgments about where your feet will land three or four steps in the future. This is similar to a chess player pursuing a long-range strategy, rather than shortsightedly pondering each successive move in the game.

Uphill climbing might seem to be the biggest challenge associated with trail running. This concern largely evaporates if you simply walk the most difficult uphill sections of a route. On inclines greater than about 10%, you'll save little time by maintaining a running pace. Instead, "gear down" to a hiking pace—and keep your stride short and fast. Don't slip into an anaerobic state by slavishly maintaining a running pace on a hill that's too steep for you; otherwise, you're ability to endure will be diminished.

While trail running, don't expect to cover ground at the same pace you may be accustomed to when running in the city. Rough terrain involves the use of more muscles, and safety dictates a slower pace just to stay in balance on the uneven ground. Furthermore, even if the footing is easy, changes in elevation require more effort. Climbing demands an obvious extra expenditure of energy, but descending isn't that much easier than running on flat ground; sometimes, it's nearly as difficult as ascending. On steep downhill grades, your quadriceps muscles will be working hard just to keep you from falling forward.

Elevations in San Diego County range from sea level to about 6500 feet, and a significant number of the trips described in this book involve running at elevations similar to mile-high Denver. If you are not acclimated to the thin air, you'll notice how easily you get out of breath, especially going up hills. The solution to this is simply to slow down a bit.

As in all of life's pursuits, practice makes perfect—or at least better and better. The more miles you put in on the trails, the more comfortable and efficient your travels will be. Running comfortably frees the mind to ponder the environment around you—the special places you've chosen to explore and enjoy.

## CLOTHING, GEAR, AND NUTRITION

The runner's key item of clothing is, of course, a pair of shoes. Hiking boots are too heavy, and tennis shoes and cross-training shoes don't have the proper tread that provides good traction on most trail surfaces. A number of higher priced "trail running" shoes are on the market, and these may suit you fine. Many trail runners, however, do fine wearing ordinary street-running shoes, as long as those shoes have a tread material and tread design capable of gripping the trail surface. Most do.

Your running shoes must fit comfortably and have enough cushioning to protect against protruding rocks and other irregularities on the trails. Since your feet will be torqued in a variety of directions as they engage the trail surface, consider buying shoes a half-size or a full size larger than normal. You can fill that extra interior space and get extra cushioning by wearing two pairs of socks.

Certain shoes designed specifically for trail running may offer greater support, durability, ankle protection, and sole protection, but those features come at the added cost of heavier weight. If you aren't an expert on issues of shoe choice, then pay a visit to a store special-

Heading for the
top of Hot
Springs Mountain
(Run 35)

izing in athletic footwear and seek help from runners who work
there.

Options for socks range from those with synthetic fibers that
wick moisture away from the feet to inexpensive cotton. Experiment
and see what works for you. Like many people, you may have a
drawer full of well-used athletic socks. Consider wearing these if you

are going to tackle excessively dusty or muddy terrain, or a trail with prickly grass seeds that easily attach to your shoes and socks. You can simply discard those old socks afterward.

If you are susceptible to blisters, try applying a skin lubricant to the affected areas of your feet to minimize rubbing. Nearly all long-distance runners experience some chafing under the arms and in the crotch and inner thigh areas. Here again, skin lubricant helps for long-duration outings.

To accommodate San Diego's County's usually mild and some-times hot climate, you'll probably want to wear running shorts and a short-sleeve top for comfort and for freedom of movement while running. Consider quick-drying synthetic clothing materials, as opposed to cotton, which collects moisture like a sponge.

San Diego's warmish climate is largely due to the area's low lati-tude (33 degrees North). Another consequence of that low latitude is the intense solar ultraviolet radiation that visits the area, particularly from March through October. Use high-SPF sunscreen on areas of your body exposed to the sun. Also, don't forget to wear a hat (legionnaire style, with a back flap covering the neck, is best), and sunglasses with UV protection.

In San Diego's rarer cold conditions, a wool or synthetic ski cap and mittens are extremely handy. These items' capability to efficiently plug thermal leaks from your body more than compensates for their trivial bulk and weight. In remote areas, you should also carry enough clothing to act as insulation adequate to keep you alive and reasonably comfortable outdoors if you were to somehow get stuck overnight.

Take rain gear when venturing into remote areas during the rainy season, generally from December through March. Even if the chances of rain are slim, a rolled-up or folded large plastic garbage bag can serve the dual role of rain protection and emergency shelter from the cold.

Again, for remote areas, it's wise to carry minimal first-aid items, and perhaps a venom extractor kit during the warmer months, when encounters with rattlesnakes are possible. A small, close-fitting day-pack, a fanny pack, or a combination daypack/fluid carrier (described below) come in handy for carrying these and other sur-vival and comfort items.

For all runs ranked moderate in this book, you'll want to carry water with you (unless it is assuredly available along the way) if the weather is warm. The moderately strenuous and strenuous runs definitely require supplemental water, as much as 1 quart or liter for every 5 miles of travel on a warm day. You should drink even more than that on a hot day. Carry somewhat more water than you think you will need, and be certain that you overestimate your need for water if you are going to be out exercising in the midday heat. This is especially important during dry Santa Ana conditions, which occur most intensely in early fall. During such episodes, San Diegans may awaken to temperatures in the 50s, but then get blasted by dry air heated to 90°F or 100°F in the early afternoon.

Several water-carrying systems are available in stores today, ranging from waist belts with pockets for water and gear to backpacks containing plastic bladders for water or other fluids that can be sipped at any time through a flexible hose. It's worth noting that the bladders work best with water alone. Sugary fluids, such as sport drinks, may be hard to clean out from the inside of the bladders.

Because even the longest runs in this book will be over within a few hours, you won't normally need a vast supply of food. Nevertheless, you should take along an adequate supply of high-calorie carbohydrate food on any trip into a remote area. Bring enough to cover your energy needs for the trip itself, plus a little extra for emergencies or delays. Do realize that plentiful food is of no value unless it is accompanied by sufficient water for digesting it.

Carbohydrate-rich, easily portable foods include dates, raisins, figs, and other dried fruits, plus the sports drinks, sports bars, and energy gels that are specifically designed for the needs of endurance athletes. For leisurely running outings, there's nothing wrong with "ordinary" foods, such as sandwiches, fresh fruit, cookies, and the like. These foods tend to be somewhat heavier, more bulky, and take longer to absorb.

A few more tips: For travel in any remote area, bring along a map and compass, and be competent in their use. GPS receivers are a helpful adjunct for navigation, but don't rely exclusively on them. The same goes for cell phones; due to inadequate coverage, they may be useless when you need them most.

Secure an extra car key to your pack or clothing, or lend the key to a companion for safekeeping. Have some kind of identification with you in case you can't get back to your car. A small packet of toilet paper or tissue may help if you find yourself in need and far away from any sanitation facility. Carry a flashlight and a cigarette lighter or matches if there's any chance of getting stranded outdoors after dark. (Caveat: San Diego's often tinder-dry vegetation is susceptible to wildfire; therefore, think very carefully before you ignite a campfire that is likely illegal and possibly dangerous. The mammoth Cedar Fire of 2003 was ignited by just such an action.)

## SAFETY

The most serious safety concerns for trail runners in San Diego County involve the nature of the terrain itself. Trails with protruding rocks, slick-rock surfaces, ball-bearing-like pebbles, or roots that resemble trip wires are all part of the immediate and generally visible hazards facing any traveler going at a fast pace. To minimize the danger, go slowly at first and take time to familiarize yourself with these hazards. You'll be able to anticipate them better as time goes on, and you'll gain the confidence to negotiate or steer clear of them.

Rattlesnakes are common in all parts of San Diego County. This is not to say that you will encounter them frequently, as most rattlesnakes are as interested in avoiding contact with you as you are with them. But a runner's rapid approach can lead to sudden encounters with rattlesnakes. Rattlesnakes are most often seen in April and May, when they may be irritable and hungry after emerging from a long hibernation. They are seldom seen in the winter months, except in the warmest parts of the desert. Make a habit of scanning the trail ahead carefully, and be ready to respond immediately to the characteristic buzzing of a rattlesnake's tail.

Ticks can be the scourge of overgrown trails in the coastal sage-scrub and chaparral country, particularly during the first warm spells of the year, when they climb to the tips of shrub branches and lie in wait for warm-blooded hosts. Once they've found a host, they search for a protected spot, where they try to attach. If you can't avoid brushing against vegetation along the trail, be sure to check yourself frequently for ticks. If you are aware of the slightest irritation on your body, you'll usually be able to intercept ticks long before they attempt to bite. Ticks would be of relatively minor concern, except that tick-borne Lyme disease, which can have serious health effects, has now spread to San Diego County.

Poison oak grows profusely along many of San Diego County's canyon bottoms, especially those below 5000 feet. It is often found on stream banks in the form of a bush or vine, and prefers the semi-shade of live and scrub oaks. Occasionally it is seen along well-used trails. Learn to recognize its distinctive three-leafed structure, and avoid touching it with skin or clothing. Since poison oak loses its leaves during the winter (usually December through March), but still retains some of the toxic oil in its stems, it can be extra hazardous at that time because it is harder to identify and avoid.

Mountain lion encounters are perhaps the rarest hazard for trail runners in San Diego, but potentially a deadly one. For decades, encounters with mountain lions were almost never reported in San Diego County. That began to change in the 1990s, due to an increase in the mountain-lion population, changes in their habitat, and other factors that are currently under study.

Several incidents involving mountain lions stalking or menacing campers, hikers, and mountain bikers have occurred in the Julian and Cuyamaca Rancho State Park areas in recent years. In the worst such incident, a woman was attacked and killed by a cougar while hiking near Cuyamaca Peak. In these geographic areas particularly, it pays to be acutely aware of the potential danger. Observe the following precautions:

- Run with one or more companions.
- If you are aware of a mountain lion's presence, don't run away from it. Fleeing from a mountain lion may trigger an instinct to attack.
- Face the animal and maintain eye contact with it. Do not act fearful. Make yourself "large": wave your arms, shake a branch, and shout. Do anything to convince the animal that you are not its prey.
- Report any mountain lion encounter to the appropriate ranger or jurisdiction.

## RULES AND TRAIL ETIQUETTE

Among the rewards of trail running are the beauty and the serenity of the outdoor environment. Just as you would not want to have your pleasant experience destroyed by annoyances from other trail users, you must yourself adhere to certain rules and codes of behavior that ensure that others enjoy their own experiences.

The hiker and backpacker mantra "leave no trace" applies to runners as well. Obviously, don't leave any trash behind. Think about the impact your passage has on the trail. Stay off of trails when they are excessively muddy, and try to avoid as much as possible blazing new trails for the purpose of bypassing muddy sections of existing trails. Don't cut trail switchbacks; this practice breaks down the trail tread and hastens erosion.

Be courteous to everyone you meet. Your sudden appearance on the trail may startle slow-moving hikers and backpackers. So slow down a bit when approaching hikers, acknowledge them, and let them know if there is additional "traffic" behind you. On most multi-use trails, regulations state that mountain bikers must yield to all other trail users, and runners and hikers yield to equestrians. Regardless of this custom, consider letting mountain bikers go by; often, it's easier for you to step off the trail for a moment. Encounters with equestrians are not as frequent as with mountain bikers, but those encounters, if sudden, can lead to disaster for a rider on a skittish horse. Stand quietly by the trailside to let the horse and rider pass.

Parking regulations vary throughout the county. Small day-use parking fees are levied at certain county parks and other recreational areas in San Diego County. Vehicles parked along roadsides and at trailheads on Cleveland National Forest lands require a parking permit called a National Forest Adventure Pass. The permit, which costs $5 daily or $30 yearly, can be purchased from any national forest office or ranger station, various backcountry stores, and from virtually every outdoor equipment and sports vendor. The permit is valid within all of Southern California's national forests: Cleveland, Angeles, San Bernardino, and Los Padres.

In the chapparal
belt of lower
Noble Canyon
(Run 43)

A similar parking fee program was initiated by Anza-Borrego Desert State Park in the late 1990s to raise money, but was eliminated after about three years due to a large, temporary state budget surplus. Because of the sudden and severe budget crisis the state is in at the time or writing, it is possible that parking fees will be reintroduced. Call Anza-Borrego Desert State Park (760) 767-5311 or (760) 767-4205, for more information.

## HOW TO USE THIS BOOK

The 50 runs in this book are organized geographically into four sections, designated as The Coast, Inland, The Mountains, and The Desert. Not entirely coincidentally, the difficulty of the routes generally increases in that same order. Coastal routes are often flat or near flat. Inland and mountain runs involve varied topography, plus hotter summer conditions and often cooler winter conditions. The handful of desert runs challenge runners with heat, aridity, and mountainous terrain.

Most of the running routes in this book are located near where residents live or where out-of-towners visit. The typical resident can reach perhaps 15 or 20 runs within a half-hour drive. This is no surprise, since San Diego's urban and suburban spaces are interleaved with spacious parks, greenbelts, and other undeveloped lands. Check out the regional map on pages viii–ix to see how many running routes in this book are close to you. The boxed numbers 1 though 50 on that map indicate the starting point for each run.

In the run descriptions themselves, the capsulized data includes the following, whenever applicable.

**Distance.** For out-and-back trips, this is the total distance out and back.

**Time.** The estimated time of completion is given as a range, based on the author's experience with each route. Competitive runners should pay attention to the lower end of the estimated time range. If you prefer an easygoing pace, observe the longer estimate of time. Obviously, every runner is different. After you have a few runs under your belt, these time estimates will be more meaningful to you.

**Type.** The route type, e.g., loop, out and back, one way.

**Elevation Gain/Loss.** This is an estimate of the sum of all the uphill segments of the run, and all the downhill segments of the run. The two figures will be the same except for on point-to-point routes. Note that an undulating route might not involve much net change in elevation, but the total gain and loss of the uphill and downhill segments could be quite large.

**Difficulty.** This specification is necessarily subjective! Some travelers may run all of given course involving steep hills, while others might walk the hard parts, run the easy stretches, and think the route is perhaps easier than stated.

**Map(s).** The map or maps listed here are primarily for further reference. When topographic maps are listed, they are designated by the quadrangle name given by the US Geological Survey. Computer software packages on the market offer local topographic maps that you can view at various levels of detail and print out for use in the field.

**Contact.** The park or agency responsible for the area is given, with its telephone number. By doing an internet search using the name of the agency as key words, you will often find useful and current information about the trail or area you are going to visit.

**Trailhead Access.** You'll find information about trailhead access and parking after the capsulized summary of each run.

**Route Directions.** Look here for a fairly succinct description of the route.

**Alternate Routes.** Some runs beg for further exploration. For those, this section gives alternate routes, or extensions.

**Trail Notes.** Here's where to find details on water and restroom facilities, hours, fees, dog access, and trail surface.

**Nature Notes.** Finally, for some runs, these comments give anything from facts on flora and fauna to comments on the aesthetics of the running experience.

# THE COAST

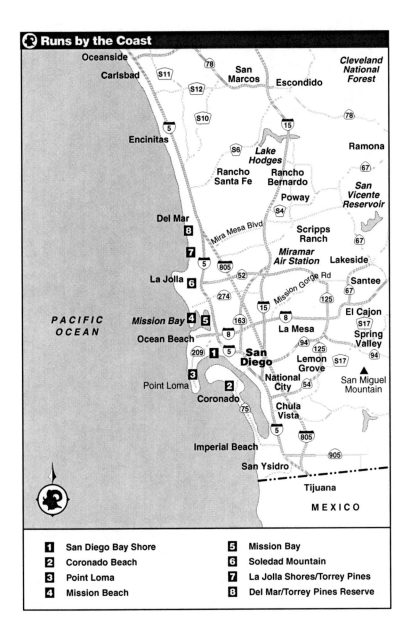

**Runs by the Coast**

Oceanside
Carlsbad
S11
S12
78
San Marcos
Escondido
Cleveland National Forest

S10
5
15
78

Encinitas
S6
Lake Hodges
Ramona
67

Rancho Santa Fe
Rancho Bernardo
Poway
San Vicente Reservoir
67

Del Mar **8**
Mira Mesa Blvd
S4
Scripps Ranch
Miramar Air Station
Lakeside
67

**7**
5
805
52
Mission Gorge Rd
125
Santee

La Jolla **6**
274
15
8
El Cajon
S17
Spring Valley
94

PACIFIC OCEAN

Mission Bay **4** **5**
163
94
125
La Mesa
S17

Ocean Beach
8
Lemon Grove
San Miguel Mountain

209
5
**1**
**San Diego**
National City
54

Point Loma
**3**
**2**
Coronado
75
Chula Vista
5
805

Imperial Beach
905

San Ysidro

Tijuana

MEXICO

| | | | |
|---|---|---|---|
| **1** | San Diego Bay Shore | **5** | Mission Bay |
| **2** | Coronado Beach | **6** | Soledad Mountain |
| **3** | Point Loma | **7** | La Jolla Shores/Torrey Pines |
| **4** | Mission Beach | **8** | Del Mar/Torrey Pines Reserve |

# 1

# SAN DIEGO BAY SHORE

It's hard to beat the superlative scenery along San Diego Bay's shoreline, even if the paths are concrete and the terrain dead flat. As much
as possible, the route stays within the linear parkland that rims the
bay, staying clear of busy traffic. The ever-present breeze off the water
brings in salt-scented air, and there's always something to look at:
other self-propelled travelers, people fishing, and various watercraft
up to the size of aircraft carriers making their way into one of the
quietest natural harbors in the world.

| | |
|---:|---|
| **Distance** | 12 miles round trip |
| **Time** | 2 to 3 hours |
| **Type** | Out and back with end loop |
| **Difficulty** | Moderate |
| **Elevation Gain/Loss** | Flat |
| **Map** | Any San Diego city street map |
| **Contact** | Port of San Diego (619) 686-6200 |

**Trailhead Access**

You may jump in nearly anywhere along this route. For convenience,
you can start where Broadway (the main east-west street in downtown San Diego) meets Pacific Highway. Nearby street parking is
abundant during the early morning hours or on weekends—especially during the off-season (non-summer) months.

**Route Directions**

Start by heading north along the Embarcadero, or waterfront, past
the cruise-ship terminal and the Maritime Museum's *Star of India*
sailing ship. Beyond the stately County Administration Center, a
landscaped concrete path alongside the water's edge curves gently
left (west), toward the airport. On the left, small boats lie at anchor,
gently bobbing up and down on the almost perennially quiet waters
of the bay. You'll share the narrow, slightly meandering path ahead
with bicyclists and pedestrians.

Opposite page:
A quiet morning
on Harbor Island
(Run 1)

Coast Guard facilities soon cut off the view of the bay, and you follow a landscaped median strip alongside busy Harbor Dr., enduring for a while the roar of nearby autos and distant aircraft. At 2.0 miles into your run, opposite the airport, stay to the left and go alongside Harbor Island Dr.

---

*Side Trip*   At the entrance to Harbor Island, you can make an optional 3-mile side trip down to the far ends of both "legs" of Harbor Island. Harbor Island—really a T-shaped artificial peninsula—was created from sediment dredged up from the bottom of the bay. It features a long, linear public park facing the bay, and hotels, parking lots, and small-boat anchorages on the inland side. You may want to stick to the sidewalk on the bay side while going in both directions. No bikes (according to park rules) will interfere, and the view of San Diego's downtown skyline rising abruptly over the reflecting surface of the bay is impressive in nearly any atmospheric condition. The hulking structures you'll probably spot straight across the bay in the direction of Coronado are aircraft carriers berthed at the North Island naval station.

---

Past the Harbor Island entrance, continue your travel west on the sidewalk that doubles as a bike path. After about a mile, a bike-route sign directs you onto the Harbor Dr. bridge, which goes over an arm of the bay. Continue west on the sidewalk, passing some Navy facilities and two traffic lights, and join a frontage road on the left. At Sun Harbor Marina, veer left and find a sidewalk that curves left around boat docks and terminals for sportfishing and whale-watching expeditions. When the sidewalk ends, you'll be forced to the right toward Scott St. Turn left and follow Scott St. two blocks to Shelter Island Dr. Then go left and continue down to Shelter Island, another artificial "island" of public and private development bordering the bay.

Now you are ready for a reconnaissance of Shelter Island, first on the sidewalk near the hotels, then looping back on the beautifully landscaped bayside path, which carries no bicycle traffic but plenty of pedestrian traffic. Alternately, you can use the bayside path to go in both directions.

After the Shelter Island loop, you will have covered about 7 miles. For the 5-mile trip back to Broadway and Pacific Highway, simply return in the most expeditious way. Go back up Shelter Island Dr., past the sportfishing terminals, and along Harbor Dr., skipping the Harbor Island side trip.

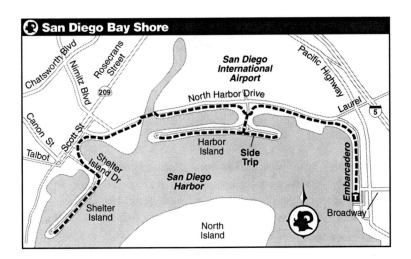

**San Diego Bay Shore**

Chatsworth Blvd · Nimitz Blvd · Rosecrans Street · Canon St · Scott St · Talbot · 209

San Diego International Airport

North Harbor Drive

Pacific Highway · Laurel · 5

Harbor Island

Side Trip

San Diego Harbor

Shelter Island Dr

Shelter Island

San Diego Harbor

North Island

Embarcadero

Broadway

Starting from the east end of Talbot St., south of Shelter Island Dr., you can explore a sandy path threading between a string of opulent houses and the placid waters of the bay. It's short—only about a quarter-mile long—yet it's one of the nicest stretches of San Diego Bay shoreline, and possibly worth a side trip from Shelter Island Dr.

**Alternate Routes**

Public restrooms and water are are available at various places along the entire route.

**Trail Notes**

The area around San Diego Bay is known for its "short thermometer"; that is, there's usually a relatively small variation in day-night temperatures. Sheltered from strong ocean breezes yet close to plenty of water, the bay shoreline also enjoys minimal changes in temperature on a yearly basis. Daytime temperatures in the 60°F to 75°F range are typical most of the year. If it's howling blizzards and frying-pan heat you crave, don't come here!

**Nature Notes**

# 2

# CORONADO BEACH

Generously wide and packed with fine-grained sand, Coronado Municipal Beach offers a short, out-and-back course that will give your bare feet a gentle massage. The dark peninsula of Point Loma floats like a mirage out to sea, and there's an ever-present view of the fanciful Hotel Del Coronado rising from the sands.

|  |  |
|---|---|
| **Distance** | 2.0 miles round trip |
| **Time** | 0.40 hour |
| **Type** | Out and back |
| **Difficulty** | Easy |
| **Elevation Gain/Loss** | Flat |
| **Map** | Any San Diego city street map |
| **Contact** | Coronado Recreation Department (619) 522-7342 |

**Trailhead Access**

Take the San Diego–Coronado bridge west from Interstate 5, just south of downtown San Diego. Westbound traffic over the bridge into Coronado slows during the morning weekday commute hours (when workers are heading west through Coronado toward North Island Naval Air Station). Eastbound traffic back to San Diego is often sluggish on weekday afternoons.

To avoid most congestion when arriving in Coronado from the bridge, keep straight on 3rd St. as you cross Orange Ave., Coronado's main street. Continue to a mandatory left turn on Alameda Blvd. After about 10 blocks on Alameda, you'll encounter beach-fronting Ocean Blvd., which has curbside parking on both sides for a distance of about 1 mile. More parking spaces can be found on any residential street inland from Ocean Blvd.

**Route Directions**

The publicly accessible stretch of Coronado Beach runs from the North Beach segment, which borders the naval air station, to the

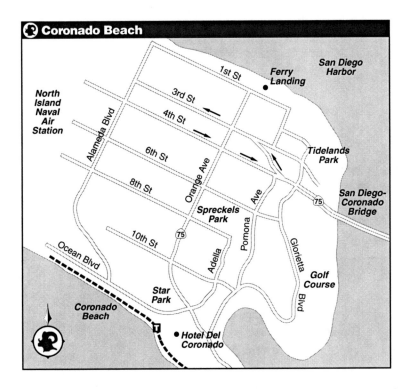

North
Island
Naval
Air
Station

Alameda Blvd

1st St

3rd St

4th St

6th St

8th St

Orange Ave

Ferry
Landing

San Diego
Harbor

Tidelands
Park

San Diego-
Coronado
Bridge

75

Ave

Pomona

Spreckels
Park

10th St

75

Adella

Ocean Blvd

Glorietta
Blvd

Golf
Course

Star
Park

Coronado
Beach

Hotel Del
Coronado

cluster of high-rise condominiums just south of the "Hotel Del." U.S. Naval Amphibious Base property lies south of the condo towers. Depending on the state of security alertness, it may be possible to run for some distance on the two beaches controlled by the military. If closures are in effect, you are limited to the municipal beach alone—a 1-mile stretch of superb, gently-shelving beach.

**Nature Notes**

Straight out to sea from Coronado, the long southward-pointing finger of Point Loma serves as a kind of natural breakwater. As a result, the power of the incoming waves at Coronado is muted most of the time. However, strong swells from the south or southwest, occurring intermittently midsummer through fall, manage to sneak around the obstruction.

Try running the Coronado beach at dusk, from north to south, on any evening when the moon is full. Between May and August, if the skies are clear, you'll likely witness the pumpkin-colored moon rising above the Victorian-styled and fancifully illuminated Hotel Del Coronado.

# 3

## POINT LOMA

The gently undulating stretch of roadway atop the Point Loma peninsula offers unparalleled vistas of both San Diego Bay and the Pacific Ocean. You have to share the road with cars for a while, but beyond the road end lies the view-rich Bayside Trail in Cabrillo National Monument.

| | |
|---:|:---|
| **Distance** | 8.4 miles |
| **Time** | 1.5 to 2 hours |
| **Type** | Out and back |
| **Elevation Gain/Loss** | 600′/600′ |
| **Difficulty** | Moderate |
| **Map** | Any San Diego city street map |
| **Contact** | Cabrillo National Monument (619) 557-5450 |

**Trailhead Access**  From Rosecrans St., 2 miles west of the San Diego Airport, take either Canon St. or Talbot St. up to Catalina Blvd. on the spine of the Point Loma peninsula. Turn left on Catalina and find a curbside parking space near the intersection of Catalina and Dupont St.

**Route Directions**  Begin by heading south on the sidewalk alongside Catalina Blvd. Catalina becomes Cabrillo Memorial Dr. as soon as you reach the boundary of the U.S. Navy's Fort Rosecrans Military Reservation. The entrance gate is open to public travel between 9 AM and 5 PM, with extended hours on summer evenings to accommodate the longer period of daylight. Inside the reservation, foot and bicycle traffic is confined to the bike lanes on the road shoulder. Being a pedestrian, you should run on the left side, facing oncoming traffic. Over most of the next 2.5 miles of undulating roadway, you can appreciate the extraordinary vistas of the Pacific Ocean and San Diego Bay, framed in places by grassy hillsides and myriad rows of

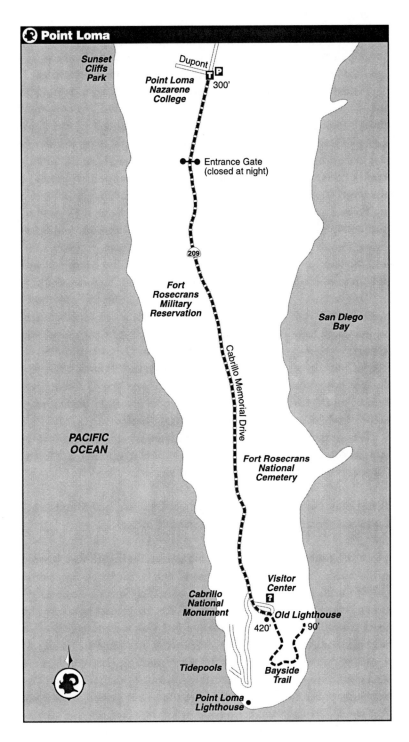

military gravestones marching down toward the water's edge. During the lunch hour on weekdays, this stretch of roadway is much frequented by runners and cyclists taking a midday break from work.

Near the end of the 2.5-mile stretch and just before you reach the entrance to Cabrillo National Monument, a road branches right toward the tidepool area. The road goes sharply downhill, past Point Loma's Coast Guard Lighthouse, but the lack of space on the shoulder makes this unattractive for runners. So go straight to the monument's entrance, and pay a small fee (runners and pedestrians get a discount) to get in. Continue to the summit ahead, which is topped by Point Loma's older lighthouse, in operation from 1855 to 1891, and nicely restored as a tourist attraction today. From the old lighthouse you can sometimes spot San Clemente Island, 70 miles west, and the San Bernardino Mountains, 100 miles north. More dependably in view are Mexico's Coronado Islands, about 20 miles south.

You've come 3.2 miles so far. The mile ahead on the generously wide Bayside Trail takes you downhill to a point about 90 feet in elevation above San Diego Bay. Amid the sweet-pungent sage scrub and chaparral vegetation, you get an eyeful of San Diego Bay, the Silver Strand, and the ever-growing San Diego skyline. Point Loma's bay slope is honeycombed with the ruins of a World War II defense system of mortars, observation bunkers, generators, and searchlights—some of which are visible along the Bayside Trail.

Where the Bayside Trail ends—or rather, where its continuation runs into off-limits Navy property—you will have come 4.2 miles. Turn around and return the way you came.

**Trail Notes**  Restrooms and water are available at Cabrillo National Monument's visitor center, just past the entrance parking lot.

**Nature Notes**  Since the potentially stupendous view from the lighthouse is what makes this run attractive, your pleasure will be increased immeasurably if the air is as clear as it can get. Coastal San Diego's clearest days occur primarily from October through March, primarily due to the drier atmosphere prevailing in that period. Rainy or smoggy periods may occur at this time as well. A north wind following the passage of a cold winter storm will clear the air as nothing else will. A Santa Ana condition (a dry wind from the northeast occurring from late September into April) may usher in an ultra-clear period, but a Santa Ana can also trigger wildfires inland or loft fine dust into the air.

# 4

# MISSION BEACH

The warmer it gets at Mission Beach, the more skin there is to see, along with much body ornamentation such as tattoos and piercings. The narrow Ocean Front Walk is the place to see others or be seen yourself—on foot, on skates, or on a bike. Mission Beach also doubles as a family vacation spot. You'll see both the families and the freaks on this easy-going sidewalk loop along the ocean and the Mission Bay shore.

| | |
|---:|:---|
| **Distance** | 3.7 miles |
| **Time** | 0.5 to 0.75 hour |
| **Type** | Loop |
| **Elevation Gain/Loss** | Flat |
| **Difficulty** | Easy |
| **Map** | Any San Diego city street map |
| **Contact** | Mission Bay Park (619) 221-8901 |

**Trailhead Access**

Use either West Mission Bay Dr. or Mission Blvd. to reach the large parking lot opposite (east of) the roller coaster at Belmont Park. There is no charge for parking.

**Route Directions**

Head south from the parking lot, past some playgrounds, and pick up the Bayside Walk along the shore of Mission Bay. This serene stretch of sidewalk is wedged tightly between beach cottages—mostly vacation rentals—and the quiet surface of Mariner's Basin. The "natural" appearance of Mission Beach and the bay are largely illusory. Both were created during an extensive dredging project during the 1940s and 50s which converted former mudflats and marshes into a shallow bay with various islands and peninsulas fashioned out of sandy sediment.

Turn right at the south end of the Bayside Walk, where the sidewalk ends and the Mission Bay entrance channel lies beyond. Head

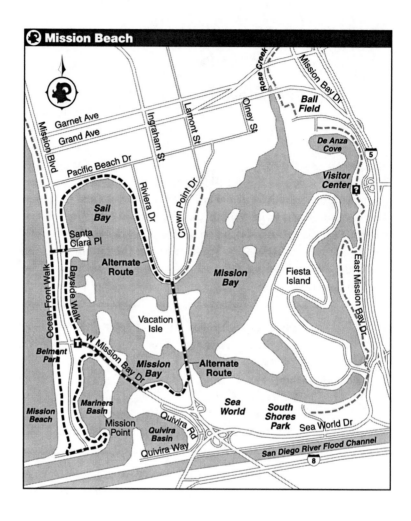

two blocks west to the wide, sandy southernmost part of Mission Beach, then go north on Ocean Front Walk, a concrete "boardwalk" with a low sea wall on the left, and a nearly unbroken line of beach cottages on the right. Recent years have seen a flurry of construction on the 2-mile stretch ahead. Formerly rustic cottages are being remodeled into two-story villas, and the concrete path itself has been widened to double its former breadth to accommodate a steady stream of foot, bike, and skate traffic.

At Santa Clara Place, 2.5 miles into your run, turn right (east), cross Mission Blvd. at a traffic signal, and go one more block to Bayside Walk. Turn right there and complete the final mile back to your starting point at West Mission Bay Dr. You can safely cross that often-busy street by going 0.1 mile either east or west to reach cross-walks and traffic signals.

**Alternate Routes**

Add another 2.8 miles to your route by turning left rather than right on Bayside Walk at Santa Clara Place. The sidewalk (Bayside Walk) circles Sail Bay and passes under the wide Ingraham St. bridge. Concrete steps lead upward to Ingraham St., and a sidewalk (divided from the traffic lanes) will take you south over the bridge, across Vacation Isle, and over a second bridge. Veer right after the second bridge, and follow a shoreline sidewalk and wooden steps to the West Mission Bay bridge. Cross over, and return to your parked car.

**Nature Notes**

Along the Ocean Front Walk, or on Mission Blvd. north of West Mission Bay Dr., you'll find an assortment of eateries catering to nearly every taste.

San Diego's benign climate produces few dramatic storms, but some places around San Diego exhibit the effects of natural forces. On rare occasions at Mission Beach, if a winter storm blows in from the Pacific during a coinciding extreme high tide (typically only in December and January), you may get sprayed or drenched by waves crashing against Ocean Front Walk's low sea wall.

# 5

# MISSION BAY

In the generally furrowed topography of San Diego County, the kind of miles of flat terrain you'll find at Mission Bay are quite hard to find. With the recent completion of a concrete sidewalk that snakes around Sail Bay and Crown Point, you can now circle the entire bay and stay well away from motorized traffic about 80% of the time.

|  |  |
|---|---|
| **Distance** | 12.2 miles |
| **Time** | 2 to 3 hours |
| **Type** | Loop |
| **Elevation Gain/Loss** | Flat |
| **Difficulty** | Moderate |
| **Map** | Any San Diego city street map |
| **Contact** | Mission Bay Park (619) 221-8901 |

**Trailhead Access**  Take the Clairemont Dr. exit from Interstate 5 (the exit is north of Interstate 8 and south of Highway 52) to reach Mission Bay Park's Visitor Information Center, overlooking the east shore of Mission Bay. This facility is a convenient starting point for the bay's circumnavigation. Plentiful free parking is available at the visitor center and all along the bay's east shore.

**Route Directions**  Head south from the Visitor Information Center on the meandering sidewalk along the bay's edge. After 1.9 miles you pass the entrance to Fiesta Island and then veer right on a bike path leading toward a parking lot at South Shores Park. From that park, head south (left) to a traffic light at Sea World Dr. Cross the street to a wide bike path running along the north levee of the San Diego River flood channel. Turn right on that path, heading west toward the ocean. The flood channel below is a prime place for bird-watching, especially when the tide is out. Look for egrets, herons, terns, curlews, and sandpipers—to name a few.

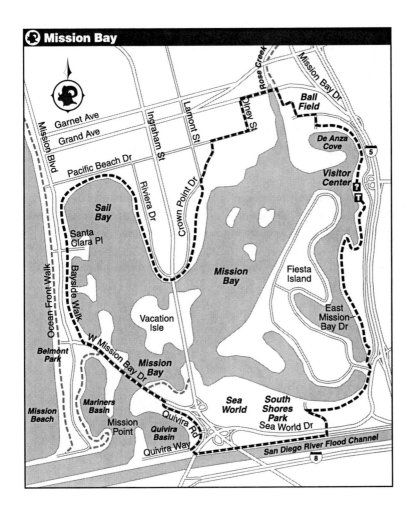

The path crosses under two bridges and connects with Quivira Way (4.0 miles). Turn right and curve north and west (continuing on Quivira Rd.) to the traffic light at West Mission Bay Dr. Beyond the light, turn left and cross over the water via the sidewalk on the right (westbound) side of the wide West Mission Bay Dr. bridge.

Past another traffic light and the Bahia hotel, veer right on the Bayside Walk. Stay on this concrete path as it curves around Sail Bay, rounds the nose of Crown Point (and goes under the Ingraham St. bridge), and ends just below Crown Point Dr. and Lamont St. (9.5 miles). Continue north on Crown Point Dr. past a well-fortified fence, which prevents any intrusion on a small wildlife reserve—the only patch of natural mudflats remaining on Mission Bay's shore.

Turn right (east) on Pacific Beach Dr., left on Olney St., and finally right (east) on busy Grand Ave.

A half mile ahead, on the far side of the Rose Creek inlet bridge, turn right on a narrow pathway going south and then east (around a ball field and a golf course) to join East Mission Bay Dr. at De Anza Cove. Continue east and pick up the bayside sidewalk again. After a short mile on the sidewalk, you'll reach your starting point at the visitor center, having completed the loop around the bay.

**Alternate Routes** You may add approximately 2 miles of additional distance to the loop above by including the southernmost parts of Bayside Walk and Ocean Front Walk, as detailed in the previous run.

**Trail Notes** Public restrooms and water are available at various places along the entire route.

# 6

# SOLEDAD MOUNTAIN

For a unique tour of La Jolla, try this unconventional 6-mile round-trip route on obscure, winding back roads. The climax is a fabulous view of greater San Diego from Soledad Park. Grades exceed 10 % in a couple of spots, so this is no easy ramble.

| | |
|---|---|
| **Distance** | 6 miles round trip |
| **Time** | 1.5 to 2 hours |
| **Type** | Out and back |
| **Elevation Gain/Loss** | 800′/800′ |
| **Difficulty** | Moderate |
| **Maps** | Any detailed map of La Jolla's streets |

**Trailhead Access**

The community of La Jolla, in the northern part of the City of San Diego, can be approached from a variety of directions. The main access road into it from the east, La Jolla Parkway (formerly Ardath Rd.), is accessible from northbound Interstate 5 and westbound Highway 52. Note that there is no access to La Jolla Parkway from Interstate 5 south. Instead, southbound I-5 travelers must exit the freeway at La Jolla Village Dr., go half a mile west, and turn left on Torrey Pines Rd. Torrey Pines Rd. and La Jolla Parkway merge together, with both streams of traffic leading toward La Jolla. At 0.8 mile past this merge, there is a traffic light at Prospect St. Go one block farther to Exchange Place, and park somewhere near the intersection of Exchange and Torrey Pines Rd. Even during the height of the tourist season, some parking can usually be found in this neighborhood.

**Route Directions**

We'll assume you begin at the traffic light at the Torrey Pines Rd./Exchange Place intersection. Start running southeast (uphill) on Exchange Place. In three short blocks Exchange Place splits into Country Club Dr. on the right and Soledad Ave. on the left. Take the

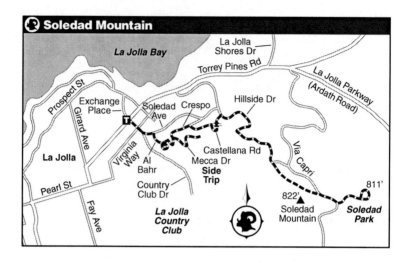

**Soledad Mountain**

latter. After one block on Soledad, go right on Al Bahr Dr. On it you pass under and then circle over a gracefully curved, arched concrete bridge. Immediately after this curlicue maneuver, turn right on Crespo St.

---

*Side Trip*     After rounding a hairpin turn on Crespo, look for the intersection of Mecca Dr. on the right. A recommended side trip up dead-end, narrow Mecca Dr. climbs to a startling dropoff offering airy and unobstructed views of La Jolla Bay and the North County coastline. Here you can enjoy the same stupendous views afforded by the some of the most advantageously sited view homes in La Jolla.

---

Look for the inconspicuous intersection of Castellana Rd., where you veer right. Just ahead, you can visit a hidden overlook at the point where Puente Rd., a stubby cul-de-sac, passes over Castellana Rd. on an arched bridge similar to the one you passed earlier. From there, tall trees frame a view of tile rooftops and La Jolla Bay.

Next, back up a little and follow Castellana as it goes under the bridge and descends to meet Hillside Dr. Turn right on Hillside and follow its steep and winding course upward along the north slope of Soledad Mountain. When you reach Rue Adriane (which leads to Via Capri), simply keep straight on an old segment of Hillside Dr. (closed to traffic). After a pleasant though breathy ramble up this steeply pitched path you reach the street named Via Capri. A few more minutes of panting takes you higher to the entrance to Soledad Park, a site that most people call Mount Soledad. Steps lead up to a high point on the site, where an Easter cross stands (as of this writing, at least). For years the cross, originally built on public land, has stood in the crossfire of community controversy concerning its identity as a religious and historical symbol.

The metropolitan view from the Easter cross steps is stunning and nearly complete around the compass. To the west, the true summit of Soledad Mountain, slightly higher and antenna-topped, partially blocks your view of the ocean horizon. After enjoying the vista, head back downhill, returning the way you came.

A water fountain can be found just east of the memorial cross on Soledad Mountain, but no restrooms are available anywhere along the route.

**Trail Notes**

October through March, when coastal skies are clearest, is the best time to enjoy the sunset from Soledad Park. Also, the sun arcs farther south this time of year, and manages to touch the ocean horizon without being blocked by the nearby landscape.

**Nature Notes**

# 7

# LA JOLLA SHORES/
# TORREY PINES

San Diego's wildest stretch of beach lies below the sheer cliffs that stretch between La Jolla Shores and Torrey Pines State Reserve. Choose a time near low tide for two reasons: first, to avoid wading certain passages; and second, to take advantage of a mostly smooth, hard-packed bed of wet sand.

| | |
|---:|:---|
| **Distance** | 10 miles round trip |
| **Time** | 2 to 3 hours |
| **Type** | Out and back |
| **Elevation Gain/Loss** | Flat |
| **Difficulty** | Moderate |
| **Map** | Any street map of northern San Diego or the La Jolla/Del Mar area |
| **Contact** | Torrey Pines State Reserve (858) 755-2063 |

**Trailhead Access**

*Southern Trailhead:* You'll begin or end at La Jolla Shores Beach (or the grassy park right next to it called Kellogg Park), which features plenty of free parking either in a large parking lot or along nearby residential streets. La Jolla Shores Beach is located north of La Jolla Parkway and just west of La Jolla Shores Dr. in La Jolla.

*Northern Trailhead:* The parking lot at the entrance to Torrey Pines State Reserve marks the other end of the route. To get there you can follow North Torrey Pines Rd. north from La Jolla. Alternately, you may exit Interstate 5 at Carmel Valley Rd., travel west until you reach the old coastal highway 101 (which is named Camino del Mar to the north and becomes North Torrey Pines Rd. to the south), and travel south to the reserve entrance. You will be charged a state-park day-use fee if you park your car inside the reserve. Outside the reserve entrance there's free parking alongside the beach on North Torrey Pines Rd.—if you can find a space.

Rolling surf off
Torrey Pines
Reserve

Let's assume you start at the south end—La Jolla Shores. Hit the sand, jog north under Scripps Pier, and continue through a section of tidepools and cobbles, about 200 yards long. By staying close to the cliffs, you can negotiate this rough area either by walking carefully in bare feet or by jogging in sandals or shoes. Beyond the last of the cobbles and wave-rounded boulders, bare feet are fine if you are accustomed to barefoot beach running.

About a half mile past the tidepools, just as you reach Black's Beach, you'll see a paved road (closed to car traffic) going up through a small canyon to La Jolla Farms Rd. This is one way to exit the beach, if you wish to greatly shorten your trip and return via the sidewalk on La Jolla Shores Dr.

Ahead, where most Black's Beach users congregate, a steep path leads to the top of the bluff, where hang gliders launch their craft. You'll probably spot beachgoers lugging their gear up and down the path. This is another exit to the outside world above, and there's plenty of free, all-day parking at the top if you want to start or end your run from there. Black's Beach is San Diego's unofficial clothing-optional venue for sunning or bathing. Gender balance is hardly ever achieved in the pursuit of those activities—au naturel males greatly outnumber females.

About 4 miles from La Jolla Shores Beach, you reach Flat Rock, where a protruding sandstone wall blocks easy passage along the water's edge. Follow the narrow path cut into the wall. On the far

**Route
Directions**

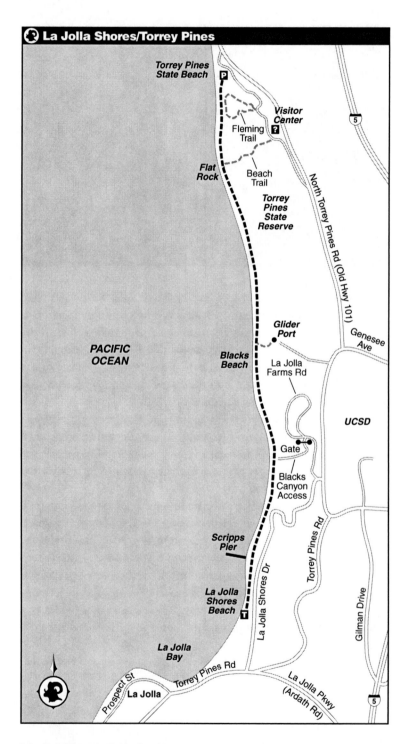

side, you'll find the foot of the Beach Trail, which descends from Torrey Pines State Reserve's visitor center.

---

The cliffs along the beach below Torrey Pines State Reserve are the tallest bluffs in western San Diego County. A close look at the cliff face reveals a slice of geologic history: the greenish siltstone on the bottom, called the Del Mar Formation, is older than the buff-colored Torrey Sandstone above it. Higher still is a thin cap of reddish sandstone, not easily seen from the beach, called the Linda Vista Formation.

*A Geological Slice*

---

In the fifth and last mile along water's edge, the narrow beach is squeezed between sculpted sedimentary cliffs on one side and crashing surf on the other. At about 5 miles the beach widens, and you arrive at Torrey Pines State Reserve's entrance. Retrace your steps to your starting point, or see the alternate routes below. With a car-shuttle arrangement, or someone to pick you up at Torrey Pines, you can make this route 5 miles one way.

For a longer run, combine this trip with a rambling tour of the trails in Torrey Pines State Reserve, or add the loop described in the next trip onto this route. You'll need running shoes for these extended runs.

**Alternate Routes**

Restrooms and water are available at La Jolla Shores and at the Torrey Pines State Reserve entrance. Don't count on finding either one between these two points.

**Trail Notes**

# 8

# DEL MAR/
# TORREY PINES RESERVE

The coastal scenery along this route is San Diego's best! Combining pavement, dirt trails, and sandy beach, this rambling, figure-eight loop will introduce you to the primary habitat of the Torrey pine, a tree whose natural range is restricted to these coastal bluffs near Del Mar and to Santa Rosa Island, near Santa Barbara. High tides, particularly in winter, may flood the beach segments of the route, so plan accordingly.

| | |
|---:|:---|
| **Distance** | 8.0 miles |
| **Time** | 1.5 to 2.5 hours |
| **Type** | Loop |
| **Elevation Gain/Loss** | 700´/700´ |
| **Difficulty** | Moderate |
| **Map** | A detailed map of Del Mar's streets may help. Free, half-page trail maps of Torrey Pines State Reserve available in the reserve. |
| **Contact** | Torrey Pines State Reserve (858) 755-2063 |

**Trailhead Access**  Our starting point is Seagrove Park, right on the beach at the foot of 15th St. in Del Mar. Parking is available on nearby streets, though it may be tough to find a space there during the height of the summer tourist season.

**Route Directions**  From Seagrove Park, head east and immediately uphill on 15th St. and cross Camino Del Mar (also known as Old Highway 101). You quickly leave the noise and traffic behind as you ascend briskly on the narrow roadway into a pleasantly wooded residential neighborhood. About a half mile into your run (or walk, if you want to ease gently into this run), the road twists sharply left and and then right in

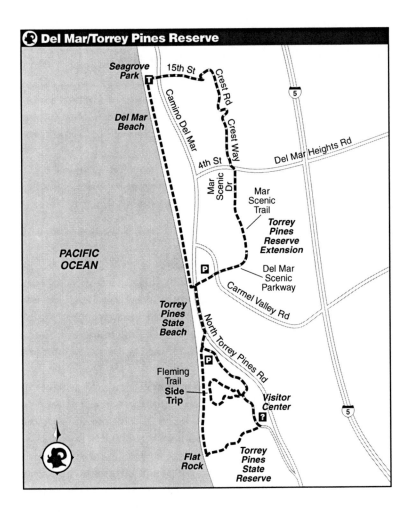

Seagrove Park

15th St

Crest Rd

Del Mar Beach

Camino Del Mar

Crest Way

4th St

Mar Scenic Dr.

Del Mar Heights Rd

5

Mar Scenic Trail

Torrey Pines Reserve Extension

PACIFIC OCEAN

Del Mar Scenic Parkway

Carmel Valley Rd

Torrey Pines State Beach

North Torrey Pines Rd

Fleming Trail Side Trip

Visitor Center

5

Flat Rock

Torrey Pines State Reserve

an S-curve. Just ahead, veer right at Crest Rd. and follow it south, climbing slightly. To the left yawns Crest Canyon, a broad ravine harboring picturesque sandstone formations and several large native Torrey pine trees. Watch for birds of prey wheeling overhead, taking advantage of the thermals.

You rise to an elevation of about 350 feet, then dip, climb, and contour to busy Del Mar Heights Rd. Cross the road at the traffic signal, go left for a half block, and turn right on Mar Scenic Dr. Within two blocks, the row of houses ends at a dead end. Continue on the Mar Scenic Trail, entering a parcel of undeveloped land known as the Torrey Pines State Reserve Extension.

Swoop a half mile downhill on this narrow path through a "garden" of aromatic sage and chaparral vegetation.

---

**The Pines of Mar Scenic Trail**

Due to their protected location inland from the coast, the scattered specimens of Torrey pines that cling to the slopes along the Mar Scenic Trail are generally larger and more symmetrical than the ones you'll see later in the main reserve.

Note that Torrey pine needles grow in bundles of five, a somewhat unusual arrangement for pines. The needles, which may grow to a length of one foot, were prized as basket-making material by the Native Americans who once lived in this area.

---

Mar Scenic Trail terminates at the cul-de-sac of Del Mar Scenic Parkway. Follow this residential street downhill to Carmel Valley Rd., cross there at the traffic light, and continue toward the beach by passing through a large parking lot. You get to the beach itself by crossing under a decaying concrete bridge that carries the traffic of Camino Del Mar. This bridge will soon be demolished and a newer, safer one constructed.

Now, jogging on wet sand, perhaps flirting with the tongues of the incoming waves, make your way south about a half mile to where the steep Torrey Pines bluffs begin. You'll note some picnic tables, a restroom building, and a parking lot to the left, just short of the cliffs. This is the entrance to Torrey Pines State Reserve (there's free entry for pedestrians). Leave the beach at this point and follow the narrow roadway going inland and sharply uphill into the reserve. This roadway, noted on some maps as Torrey Pines Park Rd., is actually a segment of the original coast highway, built to accommodate automobiles of the early twentieth century. Today, the same road probably bears more foot and bicycle traffic than car traffic. You'll gain 350 feet of elevation in 0.8 mile during the process of reaching the top of the Torrey Pines bluffs.

You'll reach the midpoint of your run (4.0 miles) when you swing around a sharp hairpin right turn, about halfway up the grade. Closer to the top you'll pass several of the larger Torrey pines in the reserve.

At the top of the grade, you'll see a rustic visitor center on left and a restroom building on the right. Go behind the restrooms and pick up the marked Beach Trail. Descend, somewhat circuitously, through a broken landscape of sandstone outcrops and deep-cut ravines. You arrive on the beach near a tiny island just offshore known as Flat Rock.

For the final 3 miles of this run, follow the beach all the way back to Seagrove Park. When the tide is low, the strip of wet, firm sand near the flowing and ebbing water allows easy passage. During higher tides, you'll likely encounter soft sand, either wet or dry.

After the first mile on the beach, the bluffs on the right disappear. If you prefer expediency over maritime scenery at this point in time, you can always hop onto the pavement of Camino Del Mar and use it to return to Seagrove Park through the tourist-clogged heart of Del Mar.

**Alternate Routes**

There are side trips aplenty in both Torrey Pines State Reserve and in the reserve's extension area. In the extension, for example, try the viewful D.A.R. Trail, which diverges west from the Mar Scenic Trail. In the main Torrey Pines reserve, don't miss the Guy Fleming Trail, just uphill from the hairpin turn in the old coast highway. The most picturesque grove of Torrey pines in the reserve can be seen on the north side of this short loop trail.

**Trail Notes**

Restrooms and water along the route are available at the entrance to Torrey Pines State Reserve and near the reserve's visitor center. The only rough section of the featured route is Beach Trail. Watch your footing on this downhill stretch of trail.

**Nature Notes**

At the peak of the wildflower bloom—usually in April—Torrey Pines State Reserve explodes into a phantasmagoria of color. The reserve contains more than 300 native plant species, most of them capable of putting on a floral show sometime during the first half of each calendar year.

Torrey Pines along the Guy Fleming Trail (Run 8)

# INLAND

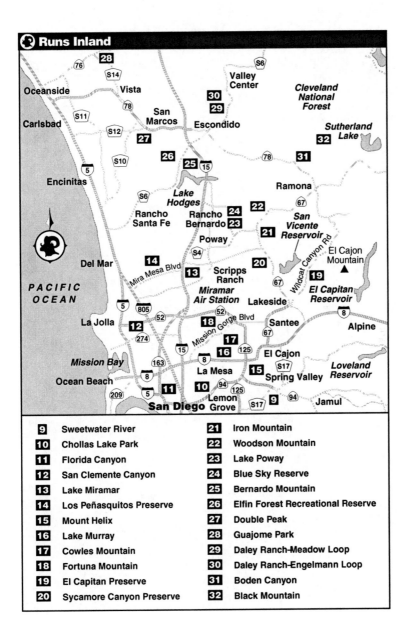

## Runs Inland

| | |
|---|---|
| **9** Sweetwater River | **21** Iron Mountain |
| **10** Chollas Lake Park | **22** Woodson Mountain |
| **11** Florida Canyon | **23** Lake Poway |
| **12** San Clemente Canyon | **24** Blue Sky Reserve |
| **13** Lake Miramar | **25** Bernardo Mountain |
| **14** Los Peñasquitos Preserve | **26** Elfin Forest Recreational Reserve |
| **15** Mount Helix | **27** Double Peak |
| **16** Lake Murray | **28** Guajome Park |
| **17** Cowles Mountain | **29** Daley Ranch–Meadow Loop |
| **18** Fortuna Mountain | **30** Daley Ranch–Engelmann Loop |
| **19** El Capitan Preserve | **31** Boden Canyon |
| **20** Sycamore Canyon Preserve | **32** Black Mountain |

# 9

# SWEETWATER RIVER

This route tours the little-known, but ecologically significant San Diego National Wildlife Refuge. You will follow the Sweetwater River through a recently acquired section of the refuge, and then trace the shoreline of the Sweetwater Reservoir on an older hiking and equestrian trail.

The San Diego National Wildlife Refuge Complex includes two units of coastal marshland along San Diego Bay, plus a much larger unit of inland territory near Jamul. With future acquisitions, the inland section may eventually include 44,000 acres of relatively undisturbed sage-scrub, chaparral, and freshwater marsh landscapes. Recent acquisitions of private land within the refuge, upstream from Sweetwater Reservoir, have opened much of that easily accessible area to legal visitation by hikers, bicyclists, runners, and birdwatchers.

| | |
|---|---|
| **Distance** | 9.2 miles round trip |
| **Time** | 2 to 3 hours |
| **Type** | Out and back |
| **Elevation Gain/Loss** | 500′/500′ |
| **Difficulty** | Moderate |
| **Map** | USGS 7.5-min *Jamul Mountains* |
| **Contact** | San Diego National Wildlife Refuge (619) 669-7295 |

**Trailhead Access**

The inland unit of the San Diego National Wildlife Refuge lies about 10 miles east of downtown San Diego. From either Interstate 5 or 805, drive east on Highway 94 to Jamacha Junction, just east of Spring Valley, where Jamacha Road and Campo Road diverge. At the traffic signal there, turn right to stay on Campo Road, which is signed Highway 94. Proceed 0.4 mile to where Highway 94 passes over the Sweetwater River on a new concrete bridge. On the right side, just west of the new bridge, stands the old, narrow, steel-truss

Opposite page:
Calm water at the
Sweetwater River

Steele Canyon Bridge, which was left intact for the benefit of cyclists and hikers. There's room to park on both sides of the old bridge.

From the parking area at the north end of the old bridge, follow Singer Lane to an access road on the left, signed 11901 SINGER LANE. A few minutes ahead you'll pass a water-treatment plant and enter a gate into the reserve. From here, miles of open space lie ahead, devoid of development save for a line of new houses creeping over the ridge to the right. To your left lies the sluggish Sweetwater River—its waters hidden by a screen of willows and other dense riparian vegetation—home to endangered species of birds such as the Least Bell's Vireo. Beyond this green strip, scrub-covered slopes fluted with shallow ravines rise toward the antenna-bewhiskered summit of San Miguel Mountain.

After 1 mile of travel, the canyon walls start closing in to form a shallow gorge; at 1.6 miles, you'll notice a large pipe, armored with razor wire, crossing high above the river bottom. Continue on the wide trail ahead for an additional 0.4 mile to where a narrow path descends obliquely left. Follow the path down through a gap in the green riparian strip and across the seasonally wet or muddy river bottom to a trail on the far (left) bank of the river. After rare heavy rains, the entire flood plain could fill with water, in which case you would have to turn back here.

Continue downstream on the left bank to where the trail becomes a fire road, and farther to a gate at 3.3 miles. You abruptly swing left, up a hillside, beginning a segment on a county-owned equestrian trail. You climb and contour along this hillside for the next mile, enjoying panoramic views of placid Sweetwater Reservoir some 200 feet below. For decades the surface and shoreline of the reservoir have been closed to recreation, a prescription that has been ardently enforced by guards on patrol.

After some easy loping, the trail curls around a ravine and stiffly climbs about 100 feet to a knoll above, where the county parks department has installed picnic tables and a shade ramada for sweating hikers, runners, and cyclists. No water is available here, but at least you can cool off in the breeze and enjoy the commanding view, which encompasses much of South County. When it's time to leave, go back the way you came.

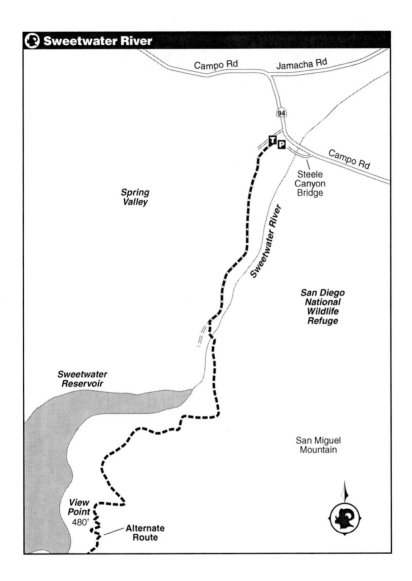

The shade ramada atop the knoll can be reached from the other direction, southwest, if you start from Sweetwater Summit County Park off San Miguel Rd. The distance is only 2.2 miles by that route, one-way. If you can line up transportation in advance, the one-way trip from Sweetwater Summit to the Steele Canyon bridge—or its reverse—is gratifying.

**Alternate Routes**

**Trail Notes**   Watch your footing on the county equestrian trail, which is narrow and often rough. Otherwise, you'll be on smooth and mostly wide trails or dirt roads. No drinking water is available along the route.

**Nature Notes**   You'll reward yourself greatly if you do this run in the cool, green, post-rainfall season, normally February and March. It's amazing how the sage-scrub vegetation on the hillsides, which looks virtually dead in summer and fall, bounces back to life within days after a soaking rain. If you must run here in the hot, dry, summer and early fall season, then choose a time either early in the morning or late in the afternoon.

# 10

# CHOLLAS LAKE PARK

Chollas Lake Park is a pleasant patch of inner-city open space, replete with eucalyptus-shaded paths and boasting a small reservoir. Invent your own cross-country course here, or use the suggested 2-mile-long route outlined below.

| | |
|---:|:---|
| **Distance** | 2.0 miles |
| **Time** | 0.4 hour |
| **Type** | Loop |
| **Elevation Gain/Loss** | 150´/150´ |
| **Difficulty** | Easy |
| **Map** | Any street map of San Diego |
| **Contact** | Chollas Lake Park (619) 527-7683 |

**Trailhead Access**

Chollas Lake Park is located in San Diego's Oak Park district, 6 miles east of downtown San Diego. The park entrance is on College Grove Dr., 0.2 mile west of College Grove Way, and west of the College Grove regional shopping center. From westbound Highway 94 you can reach the shopping center and park by exiting at College Grove Way. From eastbound Highway 94, take the College Ave. exit, go north on College, and then west on College Grove Dr. You can park for free in the lot alongside the lake. That lot often fills to capacity, but plenty of additional parking is available in a picnic area farther west on College Grove Dr.

**Route Directions**

The basic 0.8-mile, near-level dirt pathway around eucalyptus-fringed Chollas Lake keeps you in semi-shade nearly the whole time. Some athletes use this path for repeated training circuits.

The sole function of the lake today is recreation, but from 1901 to 1952 it helped serve the growing city's water supply.

People-watching along the lakeside path is always interesting, as you'll see a representative cross-section of San Diego's increasingly

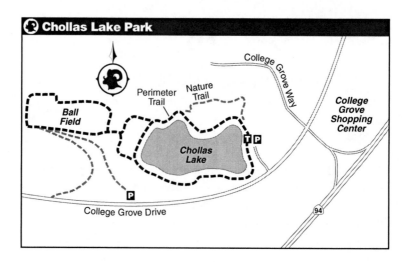

**Chollas Lake Park**

College Grove Way

College Grove Shopping Center

Perimeter Trail

Nature Trail

Ball Field

Chollas Lake

College Grove Drive

94

multi-ethnic population. Most people circle the perimeter trail in the counterclockwise direction. If you run clockwise for a few circuits, you'll soon have a nodding acquaintance with nearly every visitor.

Trail runners will probably find the larger, sunnier, less-visited patch of canyon bottom below (west of) the reservoir's dam more interesting than the lakeside path. Crisscrossed by dirt roads and informal single-track pathways, this broad bowl-shaped feature is rimmed on the north by a tall and obviously artificial berm of earth.

---

*The Dump That Wasn't* — At one time the whole canyon was slated to receive municipal refuse, but that plan never panned out. Today, planners look forward to converting this somewhat raw-looking landscape into more civilized parkland—and indeed the picnic ground on the canyon rim and a new ball field in the canyon bottom are realizations of this goal.

---

You can invent loop routes of about 2 miles duration by combining the lakeshore path and various paths in the canyon below. Throw in the 80-foot ascent of the northside berm near the ball field, and the 50-foot ascent up either side of the reservoir dam, and you have a course featuring short, steep anaerobic intervals interspersed by long flat stretches where you can catch your breath.

Chollas Lake Park is open 6:30 AM to sunset. The entire park area is **Trail Notes** fenced, with back gates allowing access from neighborhoods that rim the park. All gates are locked during closed hours.

On clear winter days, the view west from the path atop the northside **Nature Notes** berm takes in the tops of downtown San Diego's tallest buildings and a slice of the ocean. It's possible you'll even spot San Clemente Island, 70 miles offshore, from this vantage.

While cooling down after your run, try walking the nature trail on the slope north of the lake, where various native plants and exotic succulent plants are cultivated. At the crest of the trail there's a rather formidable patch of native coast cholla cactus, the plant after which the lake was named.

# 11

# FLORIDA CANYON

Adjacent to downtown San Diego, Balboa Park's 1400 acres offer a mix of tourist attractions (the zoo, museums, galleries), sports facilities, and the usual curving, tree-shaded paths you would expect in any big-city park. Somewhat uncharacteristically, an east sector of the park known as Florida Canyon remains primarily in a wild state, with a reasonable facsimile of its native sage-scrub and chaparral vegetation intact. In recent years, the park has upgraded the trail system there, making it friendly for all self-propelled travelers. The quick ascents and descents and the irregular surfaces make these trails an excellent training ground—both to increase your aerobic fitness and to hone the physical coordination necessary for long-distance trail running.

| | |
|---:|:---|
| **Distance** | Several loop options, up to 3 miles |
| **Time** | 0.5 to 1 hour |
| **Type** | Loop |
| **Elevation Gain/Loss** | Up to 200´/200´ |
| **Difficulty** | Easy |
| **Map** | A map of San Diego's city streets helps |
| **Contact** | Balboa Park (619) 235-1122 |

**Trailhead Access** The primary trailhead for the Florida Canyon trail system lies just west of Morley Field, a complex of tennis courts and other sports facilities in the northeast corner of Balboa Park. You can get there by exiting Interstate 5 at Pershing Dr., and shortly after turning left on Florida Dr. From Florida, make a right on Morley Field Dr., and shortly after another right into the small parking lot (free) near the trailhead itself. If that lot is full, there's plenty more parking space next to the tennis courts at Morley Field.

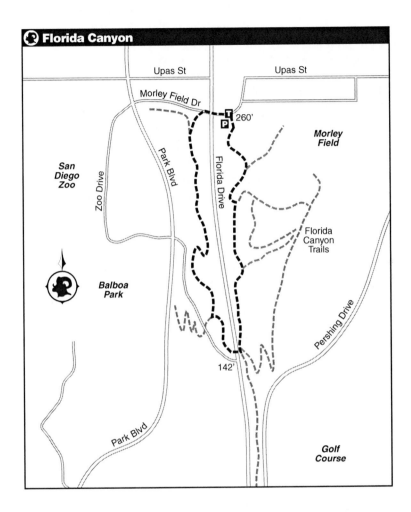

**Florida Canyon**

Upas St

Upas St

Morley Field Dr

260'

Morley Field

San Diego Zoo

Zoo Drive

Park Blvd

Florida Drive

Florida Canyon Trails

Balboa Park

Pershing Drive

142'

Park Blvd

Golf Course

The grassy space to the south of the parking lot is open to free-run-ning dogs and their supervising owners. Across the grass, the main trail descends south, alongside the east slope of Florida Canyon. You soon encounter a tightly spaced network of trails that provide numerous route options. Going left right away will put you on the rim of the canyon, while staying right leads to an easier passage alongside Florida Dr.—the noisy roadway through the canyon. Florida Dr. may someday be permanently closed to automobile traf-fic, and (hopefully) the canyon bottom revegetated.

**Route Directions**

When you've traveled about a mile south, you can make your looping route as lengthy as possible by crossing Florida Dr. at the intersection of Zoo Dr. A meandering trail on the west side of Florida Dr. (west slope of Florida Canyon) continues north, eventually returning to Morley Field Dr. Use Morley Field Dr. to return to your starting point.

**Trail Notes**   Florida Canyon's narrow dirt trails, with their irregular and sometimes rutted and rocky surfaces, require that you pay close attention to your footing at all times. Water fountains and restrooms are located close to the trailhead.

**Nature Notes**   Keep in mind that the natural vegetation of Florida Canyon is bound to appear scruffy and often desiccated by comparison with the irrigated and artificial landscape of Balboa Park's western section. Winter rains and spring sunshine almost always revive the many native plants in the canyon that lie dormant during the dry summer season. In wet years, native and nonnative wildflowers pop up everywhere in Florida Canyon, especially during March and April.

# 12

## SAN CLEMENTE CANYON

Marian Bear Park, also known as San Clemente Canyon, parallels Highway 52 (the San Clemente Canyon Freeway) for about 3 miles. The canyon bottom harbors a rare mix of massive sycamores, stately live oaks, climbing vines, and tangled shrubs. A popular trail through the canyon crosses a seasonal stream several times and offers plenty of shade.

| | |
|---:|:---|
| **Distance** | Up to 6 miles round trip |
| **Time** | Up to 1.5 hours |
| **Type** | Out and back |
| **Elevation Gain/Loss** | Nearly flat |
| **Difficulty** | Easy |
| **Map** | A San Diego city-street map is useful for exploring side paths |
| **Contact** | Marian Bear Park (858) 581-9952 |

**Trailhead Access**

There are two good starting points, Regents Rd. and Genesee Ave., immediately south of Highway 52 in each case. You can exit the freeway both eastbound and westbound on 52 to reach Regents or Genesee. The two trailheads feature free parking, picnic tables, drinking water, and restrooms.

**Route Directions**

From either trailhead, you can run east to Interstate 805, where the canyon trail ends, and west toward the railroad tracks that parallel Interstate 5. If you do both out-and-back segments, you will cover a total of about 6 miles. The main path, popular with hikers, dog-walkers, runners, and mountain bikers, evolved from an earlier primitive dirt road along the canyon bottom. Today, the trail surface varies from a single-track to barely a double-track in width, and it all but disappears amid cobblestones at stream crossings. During the wet season, you may have to splash across some ankle-deep water at these crossings.

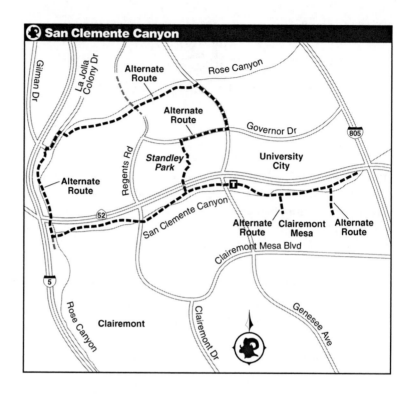

**San Clemente Canyon**

The east section of the canyon (between Genesee Ave. and Interstate 805) offers the prettiest vegetation and the densest shade—plus major infestations of poison oak, which is perfectly suited to the native wooded habitat here. From the safety of the open trail you can admire the tangled masses of poison-oak growth, which reaches high into some of the trees. Beginning around October, the poison oak foliage turns bright red in pleasing complement to the evergreen live oaks and the yellows and oranges of the sycamores and willows.

**Alternate Routes**
Although there is but one principal trail in San Clemente Canyon itself, there are several ways to depart from the norm on side paths. From a point between Regents Rd. and Genesee Ave., a 0.5-mile-long trail goes north under Highway 52, follows a sage-scented ravine, zigzags up through a hidden eucalyptus grove, and reaches Standley Park in University City. On the south side of San Clemente Canyon, east of Genesee, an obscure pathway darts up a finger canyon to Cobb Dr. in the Clairemont Mesa residential area. Another path near Interstate 805 follows high-voltage power lines south

toward Kroc Junior High School. Mountain bikers who frequent the canyon have created their own paths across the hillsides, especially west near Interstate 5.

By making use of a bicycle path just east of and parallel to I-5, you can reach a pleasant, though not-so-shady trail in Rose Canyon, the next canyon north of San Clemente Canyon. You can fashion a loop route by including the Rose Canyon stretch and then returning to San Clemente Canyon via Genesee Ave., Governor Dr., and Standley Park.

**Nature Notes**

The densely wooded bottomland of San Clemente Canyon was saved from destruction in the late 1960s when authorities decided to build Highway 52 north of the canyon stream rather than along the canyon bottom itself. Still, the freeway is near enough to contribute considerable annoying noise to a landscape that otherwise looks agreeably wild. To experience the minimum amount of noise pollution, come here on Sunday morning, when traffic on the freeway is sparse.

# 13

## LAKE MIRAMAR

Perched halfway up the dry hills that overlook Mira Mesa and Scripps Ranch, Lake Miramar serves recreational pursuits such as boating and fishing. The paved road encircling the lake is popular with runners and other self-propelled travelers. On that road you're never far from the water's edge, and the coastal breeze, sweeping inland across the water, nearly always keeps you refreshed.

| | |
|---:|:---|
| **Distance** | 5 miles |
| **Time** | 0.75 to 1 hour |
| **Type** | Loop |
| **Elevation Gain/Loss** | Nearly flat |
| **Difficulty** | Easy |
| **Map** | A San Diego city street map may be useful |
| **Contact** | San Diego City Lakes (858) 465-3474 |

**Trailhead Access**
From Interstate 15, exit at Mira Mesa Blvd., and go east to a T-intersection with Scripps Ranch Blvd. Turn right there, go south to the second traffic light (Scripps Lake Dr.), and turn left. After half a mile, you will see the entrance to Miramar Lake on the left. There are plenty of free parking spaces along the south shore of the lake.

**Route Directions**
The road around the lake is smooth, nearly flat, and paved throughout. Many runners start their circle trip by going east (counterclockwise), twisting and turning around the two long arms of the lake to the north side, and completing the loop by going over the top of the earth-fill dam. You'll be in good company on this route. Most days there are dozens to hundreds of people exercising in the same or similar ways. Saturday through Tuesday cars are allowed on the eastern two-thirds of the road, to the detriment of cyclists, inline skaters,

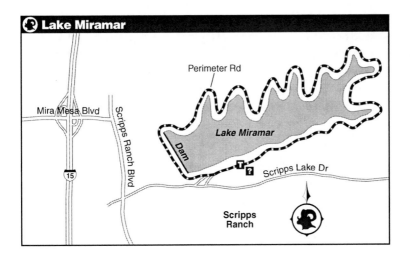

and even runners, who must then dodge more than just slow-moving pedestrians.

Entire neighborhoods have sprouted up on the higher ground above the lake over the past 20 years, but a certain buffer of natural landscape, mostly covered by chaparral, remains intact. In the springtime, the chaparral vegetation turns green and flowery, and exudes a sweet perfume that makes running especially enjoyable here.

From the top of the dam, on the west side of the lake, you look beyond Interstate 15 to the flat sprawl of suburban Mira Mesa, and farther out to the ocean, if the weather allows. The table-flat Miramar Marine Corps Air Station and Kearny Mesa stretch to the southwest. Soledad Mountain in La Jolla, and the high-rise buildings of the "Golden Triangle" punctuate the horizon to the west. To the south march the eucalyptus-covered neighborhoods of Scripps Ranch—once part of Rancho Miramar, the retreat of publishing magnate E. W. Scripps.

Note: After the attack of September 11, 2001, the perimeter road segment crossing the dam itself was closed to all recreational use. No loop route is allowable as of this writing, but you can circle the lake for about 4 miles and then return on the same route. Plans are afoot to reopen the stretch of roadway across the dam—at least during certain hours or days.

|            | Lake Miramar was completed in 1960 as part of the Second San Diego |
|:-----------|:-------------------------------------------------------------------|

**Miramar**
**Water**

Lake Miramar was completed in 1960 as part of the Second San Diego Aqueduct project. Water shipped south into the reservoir and through the adjoining water-treatment plant originates from both the Colorado River and northern California sources. Water levels in the lake are normally kept high, to ensure emergency supplies for the city, and also to serve recreational needs.

**Trail Notes**

The Miramar lake shore is open every day, sunrise to sunset, for self-propelled travelers and for picnicking. Pit toilets are spaced along the perimeter road. The lake itself is open to boating, sailboarding, and fishing Saturday through Tuesday. Concession services are open Saturday through Tuesday.

# 14

# LOS PEÑASQUITOS PRESERVE

An oasis amid suburban sprawl, 3720-acre Los Peñasquitos Canyon Preserve extends 7 miles between Interstates 5 and 15 and includes a major east-west canyon and river bottom, the Los Peñasquitos (Little Cliffs) Canyon. A 6-mile section of the canyon, free of any crossing by roads, invites runners to get a taste of what this place was like for nearly two centuries: a serene grazing ground for cattle, dotted with groves of oaks and sycamores, complete with a gurgling stream lazily making its way toward the ocean.

|  |  |
|---|---|
| **Distance** | 12.0 miles round trip |
| **Time** | 2 to 3 hours |
| **Type** | Out and back |
| **Elevation Gain/Loss** | 400´/400´ |
| **Difficulty** | Moderate |
| **Map** | USGS 7.5-min *Del Mar* covers the entire canyon but lacks new roads and features in the region. A *Los Peñasquitos Canyon Preserve* map/brochure is available at the Rancho de los Peñasquitos site. A San Diego city street map will help in locating the trailheads. |
| **Contact** | Los Peñasquitos Canyon Preserve (858) 538-8066 |

**Trailhead Access**

You can start from either end of the canyon, where you can park for $1 in spacious lots. To reach the main staging area on the east end, exit Interstate 15 at Mercy Rd. and go west to a T-intersection with Black Mountain Rd. Go right and immediately left to enter the large parking lot. To reach the west-end trailhead, follow Sorrento Valley Blvd. 1 mile east from the I-5/I-805 merge and look for the trailhead parking lot on the right. Note: A huge reconstruction of the merge and auxiliary roads will be taking place over the next several years, so consult a current city street map to determine where to exit either I-5 or I-805.

**Route Directions** We'll assume you start at the large parking and equestrian staging area on Black Mountain Rd., just north of Mercy Rd. Head west on the main, wide, dirt multi-use trail, which will take you all the way to the lower end of the canyon. This popular pathway gets plenty of use by hikers, runners, mountain bikers, and equestrians.

In the first mile the pathway hugs Los Peñasquitos Canyon's south wall, a steep hillside covered by a luxuriant growth of chaparral shrubs and small trees.

---

*Nonnative Vegetation* Near the 1862 Rancho de los Peñasquitos ranch house (screened from view by willows and dense vegetation along the creek), you'll notice several nonnative plants—eucalyptus, fan palms, and fennel, for example—introduced into this area over the past century. Ongoing thinning and elimination of the nonnatives attempts to return the area to its original mix of riparian and oak-woodland vegetation. Regardless of its origin, from a runner's point of view, the scenery is pleasant and shade is abundant.

---

Soon you enter a long and beautiful canopy of intertwined live oaks, accompanied by a lush understory, mostly of poison oak. Mileposts along the main pathway help you gauge your progress. At

mile 2 you emerge from the dense cover of oaks and continue through a grassy meadow dotted with a few small elderberry trees. Spring wildflowers put on a good show here in March and April.

Near the 3-mile marker, you are finally challenged with some elevation gain as the path winds up onto a chaparral slope in order to detour around a narrow, rocky section of the canyon on your right. Near the top of the grade, there's a spot for securing mountain bikes, and a foot trail that descends to the "falls" of Los Peñasquitos Canyon.

*Side Trip*

A short path descends north to the falls, where the stream tumbles over an obstacle course of broken bedrock. Polished rock 10 feet up on either side of the watercourse indicates the water level during rare floods—but most of the time these cascades are sluggish.

Beyond the falls area, the main pathway begins a significant descent on the south slope and then rolls gently up and down over more grassland dotted with small trees and shrubs. Large sycamores and cottonwoods grow down near the flood plain that flanks the creek.

You swing to the left, around a significant bend in the canyon (5.2 miles). Across the nearly treeless landscape ahead, you can catch sight of much housing, industrial, and highway construction activity around the I-5/I-805 merge. At a trail junction a little farther (5.6 miles) you can either go straight toward the Cuervo adobe ruins (circa 1857), or follow the trail to the left (east) that goes under a Sorrento Valley Blvd. overpass and terminates at the canyon's west trailhead parking area. Return the way you came for a round trip of 12 miles.

**Alternate Routes**

As noted in the *Los Peñasquitos Canyon Preserve* map/brochure, there are five marked crossings of the Los Peñasquitos Canyon stream going north from the main multi-use pathway. These lead to paralleling segments of trail on the far (north) side of the stream. You may want to explore some of these segments on your return trek through the canyon. Be sure to use only the five designated crossings. Fording the creek at other spots is an invitation to poison-oak rash.

**Nature Notes**   With 500 plant species identified so far in the preserve, you can imagine how beautiful wildflower season is here, especially following a winter of plentiful rains. March and April are the two best months.

If rainfall is particularly heavy, the trails can become a muddy mess, and the preserve may be closed until the whole place dries out.

Despite encroaching suburban development, Los Peñasquitos Canyon still hosts mule deer, coyotes, bobcats, raccoons, and even an occasional mountain lion or two. Early morning is the best time to spot these creatures and more.

# 15

## MOUNT HELIX

Narrow residential byways curling around the slopes of Mount Helix—many of them laid out in the days of horseless carriages—provide plenty of elevation gain on this route, plus incomparable views of San Diego County's southwest quadrant.

| | |
|---:|:---|
| **Distance** | 5.7 miles |
| **Time** | 1 to 1.5 hours |
| **Type** | Loop/out and back |
| **Elevation Gain/Loss** | 1000´/1000´ |
| **Difficulty** | Moderate |
| **Map** | Any San Diego city street map |
| **Contact** | None |

The starting point is Eucalyptus County Park, located on Bancroft Dr. just east of Highway 125 and about 1 mile north of Highway 94, in La Mesa. You may exit eastbound or westbound Highway 94 at Bancroft Dr., and go 1 mile north to get there. **Trailhead Access**

From Eucalyptus Park, you begin a mostly ascending course up the west flank of Mount Helix, along quiet, residential byways. First head north along Bancroft Dr. to Golondrina Dr. Turn right. After a long block, make a left on Carmichael, a quick right on El Tejado, and a quick left on Beaumont Dr. **Route Directions**

Where Beaumont meets Alto Dr. (1.5 miles into the run), turn right. You'll follow Alto, a paved track barely two lanes wide, for the next 1.1 miles of twists and turns up the west and north flanks of Mount Helix. The "crux" of this climb is a nearly straight stretch just before a hairpin turn. The incline is so steep that you can maintain almost the same speed by walking fast as you would by running. After that hairpin turn, the road eases considerably and you can comfortably turn your gaze upon the ever-widening cityscape below.

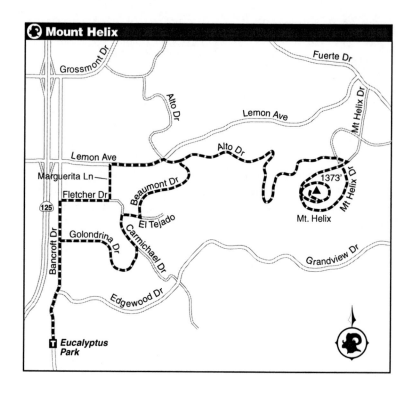

At 2.6 miles you reach Mount Helix Dr. Off to the right, on the far side, follow the ramp leading to the top of a rustic overpass. Turn right, go over that overpass, and continue chugging uphill along the north slope of Mount Helix. Modest-sized mansions dot these upper slopes of the mountain, but none as unusual as the one to your left—a mushroom-shaped structure that turns like a revolving restaurant. At the next junction, just west of the summit, make a sharp left and complete the climb to the outdoor amphitheater that perches atop Helix's summit. The amphitheater is used for Easter sunrise services and other special events. You can find a drinking fountain near the left side of the "stage."

---

*The Easter Cross*

The high point, at the top of the amphitheater, features a white Easter cross, visible for miles around. The view from the base of the cross is almost panoramic, with Tijuana easily visible to the south, parts of downtown San Diego and the ocean to the west, and ridge after ridge of mountains behind the El Cajon Valley in the east.

---

Your descent can utilize a variation on the route of the ascent, with almost the same mileage as the ascent. Descend to the junction just west of the summit, but turn left (not right, which is the way you came), and curl downhill along the mountain's south flank, which offers practically an aerial view of the suburban Spring Valley below. When you reach Alto Dr., retrace your steps on that route. Continue on Alto, just beyond Beaumont Dr., to Lemon Ave. Make a left on Lemon Ave., a left on Marguerita Lane, a right on Fletcher Dr., and a left on Bancroft Dr. to return to Eucalyptus Park.

**Alternate Routes**

The narrow, winding, residential avenues of Mount Helix are a mere taste of the many interesting routes you can try in the rolling hills both north, east, and south. North of Mount Helix, but south of Interstate 8, you can find a number of modest-looking homes and cabins that date from a century ago when this area, called "Grossmont," was an artist colony.

**Trail Notes**

The route is entirely on smooth pavement, though the road shoulders are typically narrow or nonexistent. If you run early on Saturday or Sunday, traffic is practically nil. Water is available only at Eucalyptus Park and at the Helix amphitheater. There are no restroom facilities atop Mount Helix except during performances at the amphitheater.

# 16

# LAKE MURRAY

Lake Murray is near-East County's most pleasant and most popular place to gulp some fresh air before or after work, or on the weekends. This San Diego city reservoir anchors the southern end of Mission Trails Regional Park, one of the largest urban parks in the nation. Like Lake Miramar to the north, Lake Murray serves both as a water storage facility and a recreational resource. The notable difference between the two lakes is that no motorized vehicles are allowed on Murray's perimeter road.

|  |  |
|---:|:---|
| **Distance** | 6 miles round trip |
| **Time** | 1 to 1.25 hours |
| **Type** | Out and back |
| **Elevation Gain/Loss** | Nearly flat |
| **Difficulty** | Easy |
| **Map** | A San Diego city street map is helpful |
| **Contact** | San Diego City Lakes (858) 465-3474 |

**Trailhead Access**
From Interstate 8 take the Lake Murray Blvd. exit, turn north, and drive 0.5 mile to Kiowa Dr. Turn left on Kiowa and proceed a long block to the Lake Murray gate. Parking is free in the spacious lots ahead.

**Route Directions**
The Lake Murray perimeter service road, gated to keep out motor vehicles, extends for just over 3 miles along the shoreline. After swinging around four fingerlike arms of the lake, the publicly accessible part of the road comes to an end at a formidable fence just shy of the west abutment of the Lake Murray dam. There's no passage across the narrow concrete dam ahead (completed in 1918), so you must turn back and return the way you came. Spray painted mileage marks, and occasional wooden posts, keep you apprised of your progress at intervals of a quarter mile. The mileage scheme starts back

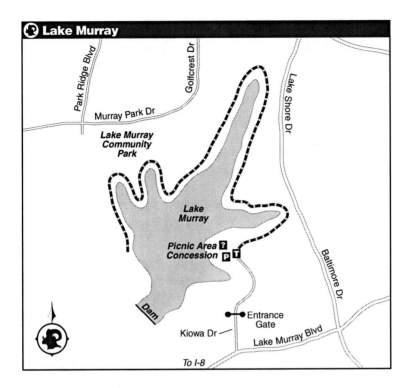

at the entrance off Kiowa Dr.—you'll note that the half-mile marker is located only a short distance in from the gate where the traffic-free road starts.

Eucalyptus and jacaranda trees spread shade over the road occasionally, but mostly this is route open to the warm sun—which is why runners much prefer the early morning and late afternoon/evening hours.

**Alternate Routes**

In a few spots, a trail will diverge from and later return to the paved main road, either following the shoreline or the slope higher up. These are fun to follow on the return leg of your run.

**Trail Notes**

The lakeshore is open every day, sunrise to sunset, by way of the Kiowa Dr. entrance. Fishing and boating are allowed only on Wednesday, Saturday, and Sunday. A concession stand at the Kiowa Dr. entrance is open on those same days. Pit toilets are spaced at frequent intervals along the perimeter road. Water can be obtained at the Kiowa Dr. entrance and at Lake Murray Community Park, about two-thirds of the way to the end of the perimeter road.

You can access the Lake Murray perimeter road from two other entry points. (This is especially useful to know for early morning or late evening visits, when the main entrance is closed.) You can find curbside parking along Baltimore Dr., 0.6 mile north of Lake Murray Blvd. and descend to the lake from there. Or you may park next to the ballfield complex at Lake Murray Community Park on Murray Park Dr., and pick up the perimeter road there as well.

**Nature Notes**   There's an active contingent of lakeshore walkers and runners who like to take advantage of the cool early morning period, starting around 5 or 6 AM.

A sunny day at
Lake Murray

# 17

## COWLES MOUNTAIN

The summit of Cowles Mountain, the highest point within the city limits of San Diego, offers the most inclusive view of San Diego County's coastal and inland regions. For runners and hikers, the ascent of the mountain is practically an obligatory experience. The following route guides you upward along the popular, south-side trail, and returns via a lesser-traveled route around the mountain's east flank.

| | |
|---:|:---|
| **Distance** | 4.2 miles |
| **Time** | 0.75 to 1.25 hours |
| **Type** | Loop |
| **Elevation Gain/Loss** | 1050´ / 1050´ |
| **Difficulty** | Moderate |
| **Map** | Mission Trails Regional Park map. A version of this map is posted at every trailhead in the park; similar maps are available at the park's visitor center, off Mission Gorge Rd. |
| **Contact** | Mission Trails Regional Park (619) 668-3276 |

**Trailhead Access**

Begin at the main Cowles Mountain trailhead, Navajo Rd. and Golfcrest Dr., in the San Carlos district of San Diego. To get there exit Interstate 8 at College Ave., go 1 mile north to Navajo Rd., turn right, and proceed 2 miles east on Navajo to Golfcrest. If the trailhead parking lot is filled up, simply park along Golfcrest Dr.

**Route Directions**

Constant foot traffic has worn away much of the decomposed granite soil on the steeper parts of the main Cowles Mountain trail. This has created an obstacle course of jutting rocks. It is challenging to ascend the main trail at running pace—just from the standpoint of keeping your balance—and downright dangerous to descend it, unless you are very careful with your foot placement and balance. As a result, this looping route takes you downhill on a smoother service road.

Begin your ascent on the switchbacking trail going up the mountain. The predominant chaparral and sage-scrub vegetation on this south side of the mountain rarely exceeds shoulder height, so views of the metropolis below are unobstructed from nearly every point on the trail (hint: to enjoy those views, either slow down to walking pace or stop!).

At a point 0.9 mile from the start, note that the main trail bends sharply left, while a narrow side trail continues straight.

---

*Tracking*
*the Sun*

The right-branching side trail about 0.9 miles from the start leads a short distance to a flat space on the mountain's south shoulder, where there once existed a circular array of stones crossed by an "arrow" of rocks. The arrow pointed southeast to where the sun rises on the winter-solstice (December 20 or 21). According to local archeologists, the prehistoric Kumeyaay Indians kept track of the sun's seasonal progress from here.

---

Just beyond, at 1.0 mile, another trail branches right and eventually descends the east slope. Stay left and continue up the slope on a series of long switchbacks. At the rocky summit of the mountain (1.4 miles and 933 feet higher than your starting point), a plaque marks the high point, and two large interpretive panels indicate and name geographically significant features near and far. This is a good place to pause and catch your breath.

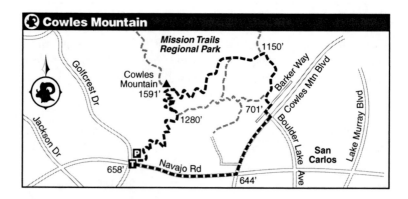

On the clearest days, typically late fall through winter, the view may include most of the higher peaks of San Diego County, the flat-topped Table Mountain behind Tijuana, and the Coronado Islands offshore. Once in a great while, Santa Catalina and San Clemente islands come into view, nearly 100 miles offshore.

Just north of the summit, nearer a bristling antenna installation, you can cool your heels at an outcrop of level rocks, and gaze down the northeast side of the mountain, which falls sheer toward suburban Santee.

For the descent of the mountain, follow the unpaved service road down along Cowles Mountain's east ridge. Steep in places, like all routes on this mountain, the road at least offers plenty of room to maneuver. You should wear shoes with good traction; otherwise you'll slip and slide. After 1.4 miles of descent, you reach pavement at a minor residential street, Barker Way. Make a right turn on Barker, a quick left on Boulder Lake Ave., and a quick right on Cowles Mountain Blvd. Continue downhill on the sidewalk of Cowles Mountain Blvd. to Navajo Rd., and swing right on Navajo to return to the trailhead, on sidewalk all the way.

**Alternate Routes**

Cowles Mountain occupies the central section of the 5700-acre Mission Trails Regional Park. Visit the park's visitor center (off Mission Gorge Rd.) and pick up a free one-page trail map, or purchase the larger, more detailed Sunbelt Publications Mission Trails

View of Lake Murray from Cowles Mountain

map if you intend to spend a lot of time following the park's intricate trail system.

**Trail Notes** Restrooms and a water fountain are located at the Navajo/Golfcrest trailhead.

**Nature Notes** A hidden register atop Cowles Mountain was once used to keep track of timed ascents of the main south-side trail. Sub-15-minute times were recorded. Twenty minutes for the ascent is still a significant accomplishment.

When low-level nocturnal fog invades the coastal section of San Diego County, most commonly in autumn, an early-morning run up Cowles Mountain may yield the dramatic sight of the sun rising over an ocean of clouds. Don't miss this magnificent experience!

# 18

## FORTUNA MOUNTAIN

Fortuna Mountain, the northernmost summit in San Diego's Mission Trails Regional Park, presides over a great deal of undeveloped land on the periphery of urban San Diego. North from Fortuna's 1291-foot summit and across Highway 52, thousands of acres of empty, corrugated land spread outward. To the south, the view from the summit takes in nearby Cowles Mountain, and urban flatlands stretching toward Mexico. This rambling, looping route up and over the Fortuna summit is but one of many possible on Mission Trails Regional Park's intricate trail system.

| | |
|---:|:---|
| **Distance** | 6.5 miles |
| **Time** | 1.5 to 2.5 hours |
| **Type** | Out and back, with figure-8 |
| **Elevation Gain/Loss** | 1600′ / 1600′ |
| **Difficulty** | Moderately strenuous |
| **Map** | Mission Trails Regional Park map. A version of this map is posted at every trailhead in the park; similar maps are available at the park's visitor center, off Mission Gorge Rd. |
| **Contact** | Mission Trails Regional Park (619) 668-3276 |

**Trailhead Access**

You start at the Jackson Dr. trailhead, where Jackson Dr. meets Mission Gorge Rd. The intersection can be reached from Interstate 8 by following Mission Gorge Rd. about 4 miles east. Free parking is available in the large lot there.

**Route Directions**

Begin running north on a gravel road—part of what's known as the Visitor Center Loop trail—that descends into Mission Gorge. Across the gorge, you'll spot some cylindrical ventilators high on the hill.

The ventilators serve an underground aqueduct—one of several in the region—that brings water from the Colorado River and northern California into San Diego County.

At the bottom of the short downhill grade, you cross the river that cut the gorge—the San Diego River—without the benefit of a bridge. The river volume has fluctuated from as little as one cubic foot per second in a dry summer to a winter record high (in 1916) of about 70,000 cubic feet per second. Fortunately, the river is almost always flowing near the lowest end of the range, and you simply skip across boulders or step across a concrete slab to avoid getting your feet wet. During and after periods of heavy winter rains (a rather rare occurrence), this crossing becomes impassable.

A heart-pounding ascent now begins as you abruptly gain more than 300 feet of elevation on the steep gravel road. It's no shame to walk a bit. Stay right on the main road as side roads branch left in close succession near the top of the grade. As the road levels out, a trail descends to the right; keep going straight. Just ahead, as the road slants left and upward, remain level on a lesser path going straight. This path contours across the hillside about halfway in altitude between the ridgeline on the left (with aqueduct ventilators) and the broad valley on the right.

You'll soon merge with a dirt road heading downhill into the broad, oak-lined valley, called Suycott Wash. When you reach the bottom, under some high-voltage power lines, you'll cross the little stream that enlivens Suycott Wash during the wetter half of the year. Keep an eye out for coyotes and mule deer, which are known to visit this area.

Continue up the other side of the wash, moderately climbing at first, underneath or just left of, the power lines. A very steep upward pitch commences, which demands that you pay close attention to where you plant your feet, to avoid slipping backward. Only the toughest runners will maintain a running gait on this stretch!

You arrive at a saddle between a low rise on the right, leading to "South" Fortuna Mountain, and a steeper ridge on the left, leading toward "North" Fortuna Mountain. Veer left and climb that ridge, beginning another killer uphill grind leading 0.4 mile to the North Fortuna summit.

After a viewful pause and a satisfying gulp from your water bottle atop the North Fortuna summit, maintain your course north on a rocky trail that descends the undulating north spine of the mountain.

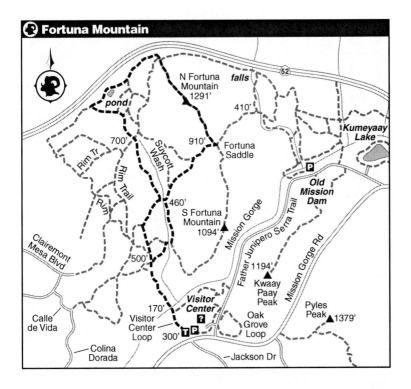

Descend to a point close to Highway 52 (ignoring intersecting trails right and left), where you follow the trail as it curves left (west) alongside the black fence bordering the freeway. Signs tell you that you are heading for Shepherd Canyon. Just ahead, more signs warn that you must stay away from the "wildlife tunnel" going under the freeway into vacant Marine Corps Air Base property to the north.

Your next turn is to the right, where you initiate a descent into shallow Shepherd Canyon, again staying close to the freeway embankment. After 0.2 mile you pass a serene little pond, fringed with willow trees, a remnant of cattle-grazing days. Continue another 0.2 mile to the next trail junction. Make a left there, climb steeply upward along a grassy hillside, and go downhill on the far side. Turn right at the next trail and head south to a saddle (elev. 700 feet) where five trails converge.

From the five-trail junction, maintain your course south, heading for the powerlines that cross Suycott Wash, a short 1 mile away, all downhill. You'll return to a trail intersection you passed earlier, directly underneath the middle of the three parallel sets of power

The shade-
dappled trail at
Suycott Wash

lines. Make a left, cross the Suycott Wash creekbed once again, then
after a few paces make a right (going south) on the Suycott Wash
trail.

　　Your return on the Suycott Wash trail takes you under the arch-
ing limbs of coast live oaks crowding the bottom of Suycott Wash. In
winter you can enjoy the sound of water coursing through the

streambed. As soon as you see picnic tables on the right, exit the ravine bottom by going right (west), uphill. Quickly, the trail divides. Take the left branch uphill for about 0.3, and go left when you reach the next intersection. You were at this spot in the early part of the run. You now return to your starting point expeditiously, reversing direction on the same gravel road you used earlier to climb out of Mission Gorge.

**Alternate Routes**

As the accompanying map of the entire Mission Trail Regional Park shows, North Fortuna's breezy summit can be approached from various trailheads: Old Mission Dam, Clairemont Mesa Blvd., Calle de Vida at Colina Dorada, and Jackson Dr. The signage is confusing on many of the trails in the Suycott Wash–Fortuna Mountain area, but you are rarely misled about getting to your destination since line-of-sight visibility is almost always available. East of Fortuna Mountain, there's a smaller network of trails to ramble on.

**Trail Notes**

No water is available either at the trailhead or en route.

**Nature Notes**

The Suycott Wash–Fortuna Mountain area has a bit of a Jekyll and Hyde personality. It can be hot and downright desolate July through October; when the rainy season starts, usually around December, it turns green, lush, and inviting with the new growth. Take along plenty of water on warm days.

---

*Fire at Mission Trails*

The October 2003 Cedar Fire swept the entire Fortuna Mountain and Suycott Wash sections of Mission Trails Regional Park. Post-rainy-season wildflower blooms may be spectacular for the couple of springs following the fire. After several years, the landscape will likely return to its normal appearance.

---

Suycott Wash is prime habitat for rattlesnakes. Be especially cautious in early spring when snakes are most likely to be out and about.

The distinction between "north" and "south" in the name of Fortuna Mountain is a new one which appears on maps of the regional park. All other maps, topographic and road maps for instance, label North Fortuna Mountain by its original name "Fortuna Mountain."

# 19

# EL CAPITAN PRESERVE

If you have the fortitude to tackle some killer ups and downs, try this surprisingly challenging route to El Cajon Mountain, a picturesque East County landmark. Your primary destination is the 3675-foot high point along the mountain's summit ridge. A side trip, with considerable extra effort, takes you to the top of the sheer south escarpment of the same mountain, a feature known as "El Capitan" after its resemblance to Yosemite's sheer granite wall bearing the same name.

|  |  |
|---:|:---|
| **Distance** | 12.0 miles round trip |
| **Time** | 4 to 6 hours |
| **Type** | Out and back |
| **Elevation Gain/Loss** | 4300´/4300´ |
| **Difficulty** | Strenuous |
| **Map** | USGS 7.5-min *San Vicente Reservoir, El Cajon Mtn.* |
| **Contact** | San Diego County Parks and Recreation Department (858) 694-3049 |

**Trailhead Access**  From Highway 67 in Lakeside, turn east on Mapleview St., go one long block, and turn left (north) on Ashwood St. Ashwood soon becomes Wildcat Canyon Rd. Keep track of the mile markers along the roadside, which indicate the distance north from Mapleview. At 4.2 miles (0.2 mile past the 4.0 mile marker) you will find the El Capitan Open Space Preserve trailhead parking lot on the right.

**Route Directions**  With a few exceptions, this route follows an unpaved road bulldozed on public (BLM) land by miners many years ago. Mileages are estimates, and may vary depending on how many improvements have been made to the trail.

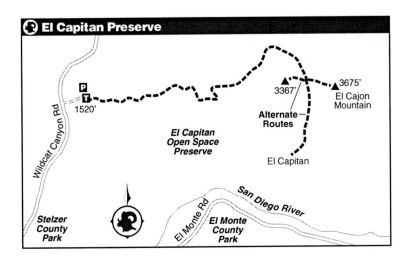

## El Capitan Preserve

Wildcat Canyon Rd

1520'

El Capitan Open Space Preserve

3367'

3675' El Cajon Mountain

Alternate Routes

El Capitan

Stelzer County Park

El Monte Rd

San Diego River

El Monte County Park

---

The miners' unsupervised road construction project resulted in some ridiculously steep grades and plenty of erosion. In the 1980s, the 2800-acre BLM parcel was deeded to the County of San Diego, which now administers it as publicly accessible open space. Currently, parts of the mining road are being incorporated into the Trans-County Trail, which will eventually stretch from Los Peñasquitos Lagoon near Del Mar to Borrego Springs, and possibly to the Salton Sea. Construction is underway on properly engineered trail segments that will bypass the worst of the steep grades on the old mining road.

*The Miners' Road*

---

At present, signs direct you east from the parking lot along a mostly unpaved access road leading to the private Blue Sky Ranch. After bypassing the ranch property and ascending a short, steep, switchbacking trail, you hook up with the old mining road. You soon arrive at a rest stop on the left, with a picnic bench and a post declaring "1 mile." A new segment of trail that swings clear of the Blue Sky Ranch is under construction and will converge with the old mining road at this same spot.

For the next few miles, you'll traverse a boulder-punctuated landscape that may come alive with a carpet of wildflowers in late winter and early spring. At about 1.2 miles, you reach a small summit and start descending; the round top and sheer south brow of El Cajon Mountain (El Capitan) becomes visible in the middle distance.

Closer, on the left, rises the impressive Silverdome peak (in the Audubon Society's Silverwood Wildlife Sanctuary), regarded as the largest monolith of granitic rock in San Diego County.

A very steep uphill pitch, commencing at about 3.0 miles, will surely reduce you to painfully slow uphill scrambling, if only for a few minutes. At just under 4 miles, you reach another significant summit. From this spot, a short side path leads north to some abandoned mines—shallow tunnels cut into a chalky hillside.

Like Sisyphus, your elevation gain is tragically interrupted just ahead. You sink 300 feet in less than a half mile on a slippery, decomposing granite surface, before once again resuming uphill progress. At about 4.7 miles, a rock-lined spring on the left, brimming with iron-rich water, serves dogs and horses (not people) that can make it this far. At about 5.5 miles, the road arrives at a saddle between El Cajon Mountain's summit dome on the left (east) and a smaller 3367-foot peak on the right (west). Swing left on the narrow, eroded, and mostly unrunnable path threading 0.5 mile and around jumbo-sized boulders toward the El Cajon Mountain summit. Enjoy the panoramic view from this well-located vantage point—midway between the higher Cuyamaca Mountains to the east, and the convoluted landscape of lower ranges and interior valleys in every other direction.

When it's time to go, return the same way. You face a taxing exercise of knee-banging descents, interrupted by two significant ascents.

**Alternate Routes**

From the saddle at 5.5 miles, you may head west 0.2 mile to an old hut and defunct antenna installation atop a 3367-foot summit. From there the 270-degree view in directions other than east is about equal to that of the El Cajon Mountain summit.

Somewhat more challenging is a 1.4-mile-long trek southward from the saddle, using a severely eroded and possibly overgrown roadbed. This takes you to the brow of El Capitan. Walk out to the edge, beyond the end of the roadbed, and descend over boulders 50 or 100 yards for a pseudo-aerial view of the San Diego River Valley and El Capitan Reservoir, complete with toylike boats floating on its blue surface.

**Trail Notes**

In places the dirt road is steep and rocky or rutted. Shoes with good traction are essential. No water is available either at the trailhead or en route.

At press time, the El Capitan Preserve, along with almost everything else along Wildcat Canyon Road, was still heavily burned from the October 2003 Cedar Fire (see p. 140). After several rainy seasons, however, the rugged hillsides of the preserve will again wear a coat of chaparral vegetation.

**Nature Notes**

Never underestimate the amount of water you will need for this trek! Spring and fall midday temperatures easily reach into the 80s, and summer days may raise water requirements to as much as a gallon per person.

Clear-air episodes can help turn the grind into an enchanting journey filled with jaw-dropping views in every direction. December through February days are often best, especially when cold north winds, or cool (only at this time of year) Santa Ana winds sweep away nearly all traces of air pollution and moisture. Days like this reveal the crisp blue ocean horizon, punctuated by the Coronado Islands, off Mexico.

# 20

# SYCAMORE CANYON PRESERVE

Sycamore Canyon Open Space Preserve covers more than 2000 acres of granite-ribbed mountains and oak-lined ravines between the cities of Poway and Lakeside. Sere and austere in summer and fall, the place comes alive with a veneer of green following the winter rains. Wildflower displays peak in April, perhaps the best month to visit.

| | |
|---:|:---|
| **Distance** | 4.7 miles |
| **Time** | 1 to 1.5 hours |
| **Type** | Loop |
| **Elevation Gain/Loss** | 500′/500′ |
| **Difficulty** | Moderate |
| **Map** | USGS 7.5-min *San Vicente Reservoir* |
| **Contact** | San Diego County Parks and Recreation Department (858) 694-3049 |

**Trailhead Access**   Sycamore Canyon Rd. entrance (open every day): From Interstate 15, follow Poway Rd. into Poway's central business district, and continue east on Poway Rd. to Garden Rd., on the right. Follow Garden Rd. east about 1 mile to Sycamore Canyon Rd. Turn right and continue on this narrow country lane until you reach the trailhead at the entrance to the preserve. Note that although Scripps Poway Parkway (a limited-access expressway) passes over Sycamore Canyon Rd., there are no access ramps connecting the two.

Highway 67 entrance (gates open weekends only): You will find this gated entrance on the west side of Highway 67, 0.7 mile south of Scripps Poway Parkway and about 6 miles north of Lakeside. On weekends you can drive in for more than a mile to a parking lot on the rim of Sycamore Canyon.

**Route Directions**   The following 4.7-mile route is pieced together from the roughly 10 miles of old ranch roads, fire roads, and newer hiking trails in the pre-

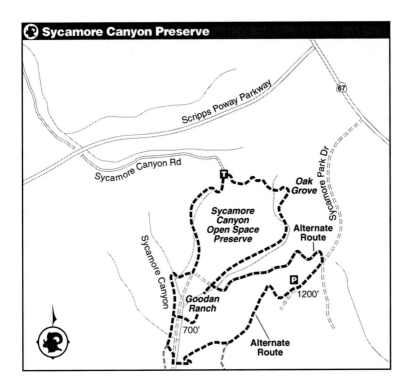

serve. From the end of Sycamore Canyon Rd., go past the informational bulletin board and jog east on a narrow trail. The path contours across a shaggy slope thickly coated with sage-scrub and chaparral vegetation.

After a short, steep descent, you traverse a ravine shaded by overarching oaks. Ahead a short distance, you pass the Martha Harville Memorial Oak Grove (0.7 mile), with wooden benches provided.

Centuries ago, Kumeyaay Indians processed acorn meal in the deep mortar holes and shallow grinding slicks indenting the surfaces of nearby rock outcrops. Poison oak is abundant here, sometimes embracing the larger oaks as if to strangle them.

Continue downhill along the woodsy ravine. You emerge in a sloping meadow, reverberating with chirping crickets near the day's end. At 1.7 miles you cross a dirt road. Just beyond this crossing, a side trail branches right toward the Olive Grove Picnic Area, nestled in a small grove of olive trees that were part of the Goodan Ranch, a piece of property that has been incorporated into the preserve.

Continue south past the picnic area, go up a little rise, then curve down and west. You reach a barn and a dirt road following Sycamore Canyon, where you turn left. Head south paralleling the trickling (in season) Sycamore Canyon stream for another 0.4 mile. At that point, take the trail to the right, which connects to a narrow, paralleling footpath. Double back on this parallel trail, going north past scattered oaks and skirting the ranch buildings. Farther on, on the same trail, you arrive at an intersection of dirt roads out in the open and north of the ranch. From there, the remaining 0.9 mile is straightforwardly uphill, as you return to the starting point on the Goodan Ranch dirt access road leading north to Sycamore Canyon Rd.

**Alternate Routes**  The other significant loop run in the Sycamore Canyon preserve is best initiated at a parking lot on Sycamore Park Dr. (an entry-way off Highway 67 with a dirt surface, which is open to vehicles on weekends only). From there, a ridge-running trail descends southwest into Sycamore Canyon, losing some 500 feet of elevation over about 2 miles. You can then circle back via Goodan Ranch, gaining back the same elevation, on a dirt road.

**Trail Notes**  No water is available either at either trailhead or en route.

The October 2003 Cedar Fire (see p. 140) skipped through the Sycamore Canyon Preserve, singeing the oak woodland and reducing much of the chaparral to ashes. Several buildings associated with the Goodan Ranch were burned.

# 21

## IRON MOUNTAIN

North County's Iron Mountain thrusts its conical, chaparral-clad summit nearly 2700 feet above sea level, a height that is frequently well above the low-lying coastal haze. On many a crystalline winter day, the summit offers a sweeping, 360-degree panorama from glistening ocean to blue mountains and back to the ocean again. The main trail to the summit is smoothly graded, hardly falters in its steady elevation gain, and is popular with all segments of the self-propelled community.

| | |
|---|---|
| **Distance** | 6.4 miles round trip |
| **Time** | 1.5 to 2.5 hours |
| **Type** | Out and back |
| **Elevation Gain/Loss** | 1200´/1200´ |
| **Difficulty** | Moderate |
| **Map** | USGS 7.5-min *San Vicente Reservoir* |
| **Contact** | Lake Poway Recreation Area |
| | (858) 679-5470 |

**Trailhead Access**

The trail begins along the east side of Highway 67, just south of its intersection with Poway Rd. This intersection is approximately 9 miles north of Lakeside and 9 miles south of Ramona. Parking is available along both sides of Highway 67.

**Route Directions**

Head east on the initially wide and near level path. Ignore the trail branching left (north). A mile into the run, the trail briefly dips to cross the bottom of a ravine. On the far side of the ravine you climb in earnest for a few minutes, negotiating the steepest grade you'll encounter along the whole route.

At 1.5 miles you reach a saddle where you can turn left or right. Stay right and commence a generally leisurely (for a while) ascent. The trailside vegetation has suffered two wildfires—in 1995 and in

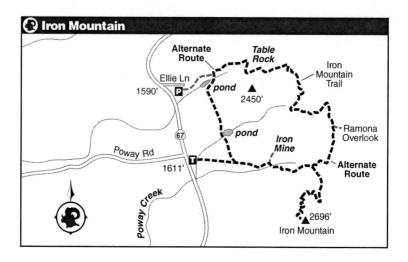

**Iron Mountain**

Alternate Route · Table Rock · Iron Mountain Trail · Ellie Ln · 1590' · pond · 2450' · 67 · pond · Iron Mine · Ramona Overlook · Poway Rd · 1611' · Alternate Route · Poway Creek · 2696' · Iron Mountain

2003 (the Cedar Fire)—and it will be several more years before thick chaparral returns.

After a decided turn to the west, the ascent steepens again, and final switchbacks take you back and forth across the ever-narrowing summit cone. On top, in a mailbox, you may find a visitor register—a notebook stuffed with hundreds of written comments. You'll also find a heavy, pier-mounted telescope (no coins required) thoughtfully placed so anyone can scan the near and far horizons.

When it's time to go, return the same way. Enjoy the freedom of your feet practically flying over a path that's almost never too steep for running comfortably.

**Alternate Routes**

You may add three more miles to your route—plus some severe ups and downs—by returning to the Highway 67/Poway Rd. trailhead via a looping path to the north. You'll pass such minor landmarks as Table Rock and two cattle ponds.

The Ellie Lane trailhead, a large equestrian staging area 0.7 mile north of Poway Rd. on Highway 67, offers an alternative starting point for the northern loop. It is typically underutilized and offers plenty of parking space.

**Trail Notes**

No water is available either at the trailhead or en route.

# 22

# WOODSON MOUNTAIN

With giant boulders galore, and consistently superb views, Woodson Mountain, also known as Mount Woodson, draws hikers, runners, and rock climbers by the score on weekdays and by hundreds on the weekends. This looping route up and over Woodson's summit includes the newer and relatively lightly traveled Fry-Koegel Trail, along the mountain's bouldery north slope.

| | |
|---:|:---|
| **Distance** | 5.5 miles |
| **Time** | 1 to 2 hours |
| **Type** | Loop |
| **Elevation Gain/Loss** | 1500′/1500′ |
| **Difficulty** | Moderate |
| **Map** | USGS 7.5-min *San Pasqual* |
| **Contact** | Lake Poway Recreation Area |
| | (858) 679-5470 |

**Trailhead Access**

Park on the wide, east shoulder of Highway 67, 3 miles north of Poway Rd. (12 miles north of Lakeside and 6 miles south of Ramona), opposite the entrance to the California Division of Forestry fire station. Carefully cross the four lanes of the highway to reach the fire station entrance. To avoid crossing the highway on foot, you may also park on the west shoulder, which offers less room.

**Route Directions**

From the fire station entrance, follow a well-beaten path south for about 200 yards, so as to hook up with the paved service road (closed to vehicular traffic) going toward Woodson's summit. The 1.5-mile-long service road has a consistent uphill grade ranging from gentle to excruciatingly steep, and presents a distinct challenge for runners who will not resort to walking any part of it.

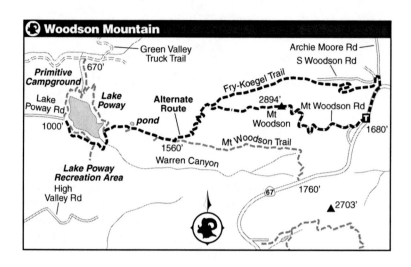

Woodson Mountain

Green Valley Truck Trail
Archie Moore Rd
S Woodson Rd
670'
Primitive Campground
Fry-Koegel Trail
Lake Poway Rd
Lake Poway
Alternate Route
2894'
Mt Woodson Rd
Mt Woodson
1000'
pond
1680'
1560'
Mt Woodson Trail
Warren Canyon
Lake Poway Recreation Area
High Valley Rd
67
1760'
▲2703'

*Woodson*
*Mountain*
*Granodiorite*

While in the hazy state of mind associated with maximized aerobic effort, try to appreciate the fantastic shapes of the rocks around you. They're of a type geologists call Woodson Mountain granodiorite, a granite-like bedrock that weathers into huge spherical and ellipsoidal bounders with smooth surfaces. Some of the largest boulders, up to 30 feet across, have cleaved into two or more pieces. The near vertical faces that often result present irresistible challenges to rock climbers.

At the top of the mountain, where communication antennas bristle amid the boulders, continue west to a point on the narrow summit ridge where you can look down on the Poway suburbs and much of north San Diego County's coastal region.

On some mornings, the great blue expanse of the Pacific Ocean blends with the lighter blue western sky. In the late afternoon the ocean glistens with reflected sunlight. You can see Santa Catalina Island in the northwest and San Clemente Islands in the west on the clearest days. Off to the right along the summit ridge look for an amazing cantilevered "potato-chip" flake of rock, the result of exfoliation and weathering.

Ahead, pick up the rough trail that tilts downward, steeply at times, along Woodson's boulder-punctuated west ridge. At a fork about 0.5 mile from the summit, continue down-ridge on the Fry-Koegel Trail, ignoring the left branch, which descends toward the Mount Woodson Trail and Lake Poway. The Fry-Koegel Trail obliquely dives down through wildly tangled, mature chaparral,

Weathered granodiorite on Woodson Mountain

bound for the Mount Woodson Estates subdivision at the north base of the mountain. Near the bottom, the trail meanders through spooky clusters of coast live oaks. Watch out for copious growths of poison oak here.

Emerging from the trees, the trail executes a circuitous switch-backing detour so as to swing around a block of residences. Then it's a straight shot to Archie Moore Rd., near Highway 67. Use that road, followed by a short segment of the Highway 67 shoulder, to return to your car.

**Alternate Routes**  A somewhat longer and more difficult climb of Woodson Mountain, 7.2 miles out and back with 2300 feet of elevation gains and losses, can be initated at Lake Poway. After contouring around the south side of the lake, turn east on the relentlessly uphill Mount Woodson Trail. After gaining about 500 feet in elevation, veer left and keep climbing on a trail branching left (north) toward Woodson's west ridge. Once you reach that west ridge, follow the ridgeline all the way up to Woodson's summit. This alternate route, through mostly low-growing chaparral and mid-sized boulders, offers excellent views but little shade.

**Trail Notes**  Every Woodson Mountain trail is steep and rocky or rutted in places, so be sure to wear shoes with good traction. No water is available either at the Highway 67 trailhead or en route.

**Nature Notes**  Woodson's summit, offering vistas to the west and east, is a superb vantage point for viewing the sun's descent into the ocean and the full moon's rise over the mountains to the east. On full-moon occasions, these two events occur nearly simultaneously. If your goal is to be on the summit at sunset on a night of the full moon, then reverse the direction of the loop route described above. When you descend the paved service road, the rising full moon will help light your way if you've lingered on the summit until dark.

# 23

# LAKE POWAY

Sixty-acre Lake Poway has served as a recreational destination for boating, fishing, hiking, and mountain biking for nearly two decades, in addition to its role as an emergency water supply for northern San Diego County. The 2.5-mile route circling the lake, a mixture of dirt roads and narrower trails, is perfect for a bit of running exercise after work or on a lazy weekend.

| | |
|---:|:---|
| **Distance** | 2.5 miles |
| **Time** | 0.5 to 1 hour |
| **Type** | Loop |
| **Elevation Gain/Loss** | 400'/400' |
| **Difficulty** | Easy |
| **Map** | USGS 7.5-min *Escondido* |
| **Contact** | Lake Poway Recreation Area |
| | (858) 679-5470 |

**Trailhead Access**

Take Rancho Bernardo Rd. east from Interstate 15. It becomes Espola Rd. at Poway's city limit. About 3 miles east of I-15, Espola Rd. bends right and continues south. Go an additional half mile and turn left on Lake Poway Rd., which leads directly to Lake Poway and its shoreline recreational area.

**Route Directions**

To go clockwise around the lake, pick up the trail beyond the entrance, on the left (north) side of the developed park area. Along the path ahead, you'll pass through four distinct plant communities— sage scrub, chaparral, oak woodland, and riparian woodland—all exemplary of the county's rocky foothills. You begin among sage scrub and chaparral as you traverse above the west shoreline and drop sharply on switchbacks to a point below the rock-fill dam. There, you meet and briefly follow a wider trail that heads downhill toward a walk-in campground and farther to the Blue Sky Ecological

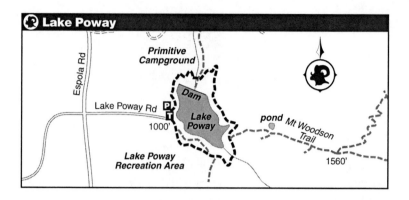

Reserve. You, however, turn right onto a path that zigzags upward for some 200 feet of elevation gain. That short but heart-pounding ascent puts you back above the level of the water in the reservoir.

You now start curling around the lake's east shore on a wider path. The Mount Woodson Trail branches left and you stay on the lakeshore path, dipping to cross the cool, damp-smelling floor of Warren Canyon, with its mini-oasis of riparian vegetation. Continue all the way around the shoreline to the grassy picnic area, boat dock, and parking lot at the lake's entrance, thereby completing your loop.

**Alternate Routes**   You can use the Lake Poway loop trail as a springboard for trips east toward Woodson Mountain, or north into the Blue Sky Ecological Reserve. See Runs 22 and 24 for more details.

**Trail Notes**   Lake Poway Recreation Area opens every day (sunrise to sunset) for trail use and picnicking. The lake itself is open Wednesday through Sunday for fishing and boating. There is a $4 parking fee for non-Poway residents, but only when attendants are on duty to collect the fee (usually on weekends).

# 24

# BLUE SKY RESERVE

The 700-acre Blue Sky Ecological Reserve near Poway protects one of the finer examples of riparian vegetation in Southern California. An important site for nature education and habitat preservation, Blue Sky is one of the most popular of the 119 California Department of Fish and Game wildlife reserves in the state. Motorized vehicles and mountain bikes are banned, so you'll be assured of peace and quiet—and more frequent wildlife sightings—while running here.

The first segment of this run follows a level trail for more than a mile. You pass under the overarching limbs of coast live oaks and edge a small stream, densely shaded by willows and other water-loving plants. Then the fun begins: a stiff climb up a sunny slope to the north, ending at the Ramona Reservoir dam.

| | |
|---|---|
| **Distance** | 5.0 miles round trip |
| **Time** | 1.25 to 2 hours |
| **Type** | Out and back |
| **Elevation Gain/Loss** | 800´/800´ |
| **Difficulty** | Moderate |
| **Map** | USGS 7.5-min *Escondido* |
| **Contact** | Blue Sky Ecological Reserve |
| | (858) 679-5469 |

**Trailhead Access**

Take Rancho Bernardo Rd. east from Interstate 15. It becomes Espola Rd. at Poway's city limit. About 3 miles east from I-15, Espola Rd. bends right and continues south. As you complete the bend, turn left into the Blue Sky Ecological Reserve trailhead parking lot.

**Route Directions**

On foot, follow the unpaved Green Valley Truck Trail eastward from Espola Rd. Traffic noise quickly disappears, and frogs hopping along the nearby creek entertain you with their guttural serenades. You run beneath spreading live oaks, with willows, sycamores, and dense

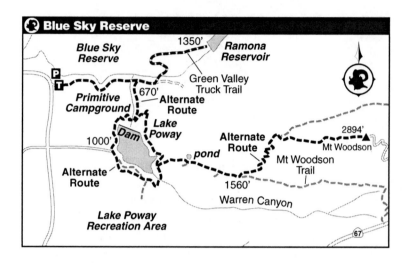

**Blue Sky Reserve**

Blue Sky Reserve

1350'

Ramona Reservoir

P T

Primitive Campground

670'

Green Valley Truck Trail

Alternate Route

1000'

Dam

Lake Poway

Alternate Route

pond

2894'

Mt Woodson

Mt Woodson Trail

Alternate Route

1560'

Warren Canyon

Lake Poway Recreation Area

67

growths of poison oak closer to the creek on your left. About a quarter mile out, a side path branches left toward the creek itself and later
returns to the main dirt road. Beware of poison oak if you follow this
or other narrow pathways in the reserve!

At 1.0 mile, a trail branching right (south) heads uphill to join the
trail system of the Lake Poway Recreation Area. Your trail splits about
0.2 mile farther, where powerlines pass overhead. Follow the left
branch (Green Valley Truck Trail), as it fords the creek and starts
climbing a dry south slope toward the Ramona Reservoir dam. In
the next 1.3 miles of steady ascent, you gain about 700 feet of elevation and enjoy an ever-expanding view of Poway, Rancho Bernardo,
and much of the remainder of inland North County's rapidly urban-
izing region. Once you reach the dam you can turn around and
return on the same route in much less time.

**Alternate Routes**  Starting from the Blue Sky trailhead, you can fashion a round-trip
run of 5.5 miles by using the connector trail to Lake Poway men-
tioned above and circling the lake on the perimeter trail. Also from
the Blue Sky trailhead, you can do a challenging 10-mile run to-
and-from Mount Woodson's summit, utilizing a steep approach up
the mountain's southwestern flank. See the map for details.

**Trail Notes**  No water is available either at the Highway 67 trailhead or en route.

After a wet winter, usually by March, the floodplain alongside the creek turns an almost unbelievably bright shade of green. Mosses, ferns, annual grasses, and fresh new shrub growth coats everything, even the rocks. More than 100 kinds of wildflowers have been identified here in a single year, mostly during April and May.

# 25

# BERNARDO MOUNTAIN

Lake Hodges has become the most popular recreation destination in the 55-mile-long San Dieguito River Park, now taking form along the San Dieguito River watershed from the coast at Del Mar to the Volcan Mountains near Julian. Trails along the Lake Hodges shoreline have long been popular, and now a route up Bernardo Mountain is attracting attention as well. In 2002, the bulk of the mountain was purchased for inclusion in the park, so now travelers can reach the top without leaving public land. The view from the top of the mountain encompasses much of the sparkling surface of Lake Hodges and includes a glimpse of the ocean.

| | |
|---:|:---|
| **Distance** | 7.2 miles round trip |
| **Time** | 1.5 to 2 hours |
| **Type** | Out and back |
| **Elevation Gain/Loss** | 1000´/1000´ |
| **Difficulty** | Moderate |
| **Map** | USGS 7.5-min *Escondido* |
| **Contact** | San Dieguito River Park (858) 674-2270 |

**Trailhead Access**  From Interstate 15, exit at Via Rancho Parkway. Go east one block to Sunset Dr., and continue driving to its end, where you'll find plenty of free parking.

**Route Directions**  Head south, parallel to the freeway, on the Coast to Crest Trail, initially a wide, concrete walkway. After about 0.4 mile, the pathway turns sharply right and passes under the I-15 bridge that goes over the east arm of Lake Hodges. Depending on the amount of rainfall over the past year or two, the lake (a San Diego city reservoir) might be brimming with water at this spot, or be completely dry, as it was in the early years of this decade. At the time of this writing, a foot/

A balanced rock
sculpture atop
Bernardo
Mountain

bicycle bridge across the water, on the west side of the freeway, is
slated for imminent construction.

On the far side of the freeway, the Coast to Crest Trail swings
north and joins for a short time the crumbling pavement of the
long-abandoned Highway 395, the former inland highway running
north from San Diego into Riverside County. Soon, however, the

pavement disappears and you're on a dirt trail going west along the shoreline. At 1.5 miles into the run, you cross Felicita Creek, a small perennial brook deeply shaded by oaks, sycamores, palms, and other water-loving vegetation.

You climb out of the creekbed and ascend moderately, wrapping around the broad flank of Bernardo Mountain. The sunny slope on the right hosts an eye-popping assortment of wildflowers March through May.

---

*Bird-Watching on the Run*  Look for snow-white egrets parasailing over the wind-rippled surface of Lake Hodges. Overhead, you'll often see hawks and ravens riding on thermals as they patrol the afternoon skies. Ospreys and golden eagles have been seen in this area as well—not to mention small and circumspect California gnatcatchers, which are classified as an endangered species.

---

At 1.7 miles, a couple of minutes past the creek crossing, make a very sharp right turn on the path heading north. You ascend slowly, with the oaks and sycamores of Felicita Creek just below you on the right and Bernardo Mountain rising on the left. By about 2.5 miles, you've swung around to the north side of the mountain, where the chaparral vegetation becomes jungle-like in density and the ascent quickens. Stay left (uphill) at the next two trail intersections, always heading upward.

You continue either rising or contouring in a zigzag pattern, passing a large water tank at 3.2 miles, and finally reaching the rocky summit at 3.6 miles. From this noble vantage point, the patchwork of urban/suburban/wildland that inland North County has become spreads before you. The white noise of traffic on Interstate 15 wafts upward, but in other directions you see little apparent human impact on the landscape. Westward, down the valley below Lake Hodges, you may see a slice of Pacific Ocean on clear days.

To complete this run, return on the same route that brought you here.

*Alternate Routes*  The Coast to Crest Trail is an uncompleted 55-mile route from San Dieguito Lagoon in Del Mar to the crest of the Volcan Mountains near Julian. The longest continuous section existing so far centers on Lake Hodges and the San Pasqual Valley to the east. Here are more options for exploring that trail:

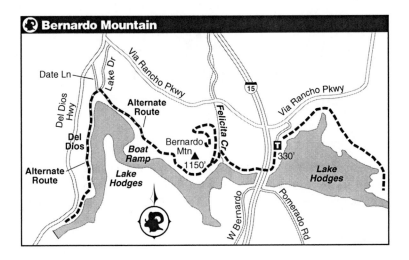

Bernardo Mountain

Instead of turning right on the cutoff to Bernardo Mountain at 1.7 miles (described in the featured run), continue west on the Coast to Crest trail for another 1.7 miles to the boat ramp and concession on the Lake Hodges shoreline. You can tank up on water here, and have a bite to eat from the snack shop (Friday through Sunday only). This makes for an easier run than the Bernardo Mountain climb.

West of the boat ramp, a less scenic segment of the Coast to Crest Trail parallels an access road for a mile, and then sticks close to the shoreline, bordering the rustic community of Del Dios. Still farther it joins a dirt road, open to auto traffic and popular among sailboard enthusiasts, who launch their craft near the lower end of the reservoir. Plans are afoot to extend the trail, as a public right-of-way, past the dam and down the gorge of the San Dieguito River toward Rancho Santa Fe.

Starting at the Sunset Dr. trailhead, a recently opened 10-mile stretch of the Coast to Crest Trail goes east into and along the San Pasqual Valley, an agricultural preserve within San Diego's city limits. Most runners will find this section a bit tedious due to long sections of trail that simply follow rural roads. Mountain bikers definitely fare better there since on wheels it's relatively flat and fast.

No water is available along the route to Bernardo Mountain.          **Trail Notes**

# 26

## ELFIN FOREST
## RECREATIONAL RESERVE

Most of the trails in the rolling, chaparral-covered uplands of the Elfin Forest Recreational Reserve branch forth from the top of a heart-poundingly steep entry path called The Way Up Trail. The upper trails are rewarding on clear days, when you can gaze across many miles of coastal landscape—increasingly but not totally crowded with houses and subdivisions. The 750-acre reserve was opened to the public in December 1992, several years before construction began on a reservoir on the south half of the site. Today, about 10 miles of the original 17 miles of roads and multi-use trail remain open during construction, and some may be modified or put back in service when the reservoir is completed. All are suitable for running.

| | |
|---:|:---|
| **Distance** | 4 or more miles |
| **Time** | 1 hour or more |
| **Type** | Out and back, with optional loops |
| **Elevation Gain/Loss** | 700 feet or more |
| **Difficulty** | Moderate |
| **Map** | Elfin Forest Recreational Reserve map/brochure, available at the trailhead |
| **Contact** | Olivenhain Municipal Water District (760) 753-6466 x147 |

**Trailhead Access**  You'll find the well-marked entrance to Elfin Forest Recreation Area near mile 6 on Harmony Grove Rd., 3 miles west of the outskirts of Escondido. Use a detailed map of North County city streets for navigating there along several possible routes. You may also drive directly to the trailhead from the coastal area (Carlsbad). From Rancho Santa Fe Rd. in eastern Carlsbad, follow Questhaven, Elfin Forest, and Harmony Grove roads east a total of 5 miles to the recreation area entrance. Again, a detailed city map will help, as a great deal of housing contruction and street realignment is taking place along the way.

**Elfin Forest Recreational Reserve**

Harmony Grove Rd

Botanical Trail

Alternate Route

492'

Escondido Creek

The Way Up Trail

Elfin
Forest
Recreational
Reserve

Escondido
Overlook
1200'

Alternate
Route

Equine Incline Trail

Ridge Top
Picnic Area

1346'
Elfin
Forest
Overlook

Reservoir
Inundation
Area

Tyke's Hike Trail

From the parking lot find and follow The Way Up Trail, up and up.

**Route Directions**

*Going Botanical*

Use the Botanical Trail instead of The Way Up Trail for a half-mile diversion with hardly any additional elevation gain. The Botanical Trail features riparian vegetation and live-oak woods along the flood plain of Escondido Creek. The wildflowers along this stretch are spectacular after a wet winter.

On the upper part of The Way Up Trail, a crooked ascent takes you up a canyon wall studded with tooth-like rock outcrops and dripping with thick, almost jungle-like growths of chaparral. In cool, wet months, the scenery and mood are friendly, but they can be somewhat grim during the hot summer, especially at midday. Looking north across the canyon, you can still see the results of the October 1996 Harmony Grove Fire, which spared all property within the reserve.

The shadeless Ridge Top Picnic Area, with restrooms and drinking water available, comes into view after 1.5 miles and 700 feet of climbing via The Way Up Trail. Of the several possibilities for pressing on from the picnic area, here's one recommendation: From the west side of the picnic area climb to Elfin Forest Overlook, which lies at the top of the ridge to the southwest. On clear days, you can look down the valley of Escondido Creek to San Elijo Lagoon and the ocean, 9 miles away. You can return to the picnic area either the same way or on a paralleling trail, and climb to another vista point overlooking Escondido. Or you can travel the long and winding Equine Incline Trail before returning back down The Way Up Trail. The latter option, coupled with the "way up" and the "way down" segments, totals about 6 miles.

**Trail Notes**   The recreation area is open daily, from 8 AM to 30 minutes before sunset, with free parking. Restrooms and drinking water are at the trailhead and at Ridge Top Picnic Area. Dogs are allowed off leash on the trails if under full control of their owners. Dogs must be leashed in parking, picnic, and overlook areas.

**Nature Notes**   Elfin Forest Recreational Reserve is the place to go if you love running with your dog. Dogs are allowed on the trails—off leash, surprisingly, as long as they are kept under full control. Hopefully, with the continued courtesy and consideration of dog owners, this policy will continue.

# 27

# DOUBLE PEAK

South of the spreading suburbs of San Marcos, a scruffy ridgeline scrapes the southern sky. Topographic maps note the obscure names of its various high points: Cerro de las Posas, Double Peak, Franks Peak, and Mount Whitney (not *that* Whitney, but still, it's the highest of the group). Double Peak lies within a future San Marcos regional park atop the ridge. Currently there's public access to Double Peak on a route utilizing old fire roads and newer trails. The summit offers one of the best panoramas of inland North County's mix of wild spaces and spreading suburbs.

| | |
|---:|:---|
| **Distance** | 5.0 miles round trip |
| **Time** | 1 to 2 hours |
| **Type** | Out and back |
| **Elevation Gain/Loss** | 1000´/1000´ |
| **Difficulty** | Moderate |
| **Map** | USGS 7.5-min *Rancho Santa Fe* |
| **Contact** | San Marcos Community Services Department (760) 744-9000 |

**Trailhead Access**

From Highway 78 in San Marcos, exit at Twin Oaks Valley Rd. Go a short mile to Craven Rd., turn right, and go another short mile to Foxhall Dr., where you turn left. Foxhall Dr. takes you to Lakeview Park, which is the starting point for the run.

**Route Directions**

On foot, cross the dam of bantam-sized Discovery Lake, and labor upward on a paved, traffic-free access road which goes 0.7 mile to a large, hillside water tank. Continue your ascent on the rough dirt road to the left, zigzagging upward through chaparral vegetation now recovering from the October 1996 Harmony Grove Fire.

At the next trail intersection (1.2 miles), turn sharply right and continue climbing more moderately to a wide fire road atop the Cerro de las Posas ridge (1.6 miles). Make a left there (southeast), dip slightly to cross a saddle, and start climbing again. Stay left at the next

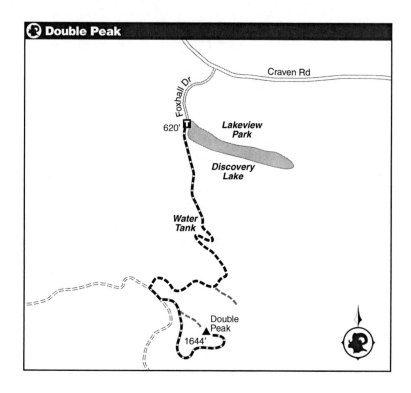

**Double Peak**

Craven Rd

Foxhall Dr

620'

*Lakeview Park*

*Discovery Lake*

*Water Tank*

Double Peak

1644'

fork in the fire road. Double Peak, fringed with a clump of trees, lies ahead. Continue on the ascending fire road, which curls around the south side of the peak and gradually approaches the peak from the back (east) side. (Note that a steep, eroded, bulldozed path goes straight up the west side of the peak—it could be used as a shortcut to the top, though it's virtually unrunnable.)

When it's time to go, return the way you came.

*At the Summit*    A messy old homesite lies atop the Double Peak summit, along with scattered eucalyptus and olive trees, and other surviving decorative landscaping. In time, the site will be doubtless be cleaned up. On clear days, let your eyes feast on the view, which stretches from the highest mountain ranges of southern California (San Gabriels, San Bernardinos, San Jacintos) in the north, to the shining Pacific Ocean in the west and southwest.

**Alternate Routes**    Old jeep trails and narrower paths lace the hilly landscape around Double Peak, and you could spend hours exploring them. Some are on future City of San Marcos park land; others enter private (and sometimes unposted) land that will likely be sold and developed for luxury housing. Enjoy these trails while you can; but please observe any No Trespassing signs.

No water is available once you are past Lakeview Park. **Trail Notes**

# 28

# GUAJOME PARK

With a mix of wild and civilized features, coastal North County's largest (though not huge) urban park, Guajome Regional Park, has become an oasis of open space amid Oceanside's rapidly spreading suburban development. Guajome's 4-mile trail system encircles cat-tail-fringed Guajome Lake and visits a small pond hidden in a secluded back corner of the park. The park's topography is gentle hills, making its trails ideal for jogging.

| | |
|---:|:---|
| **Distance** | Up to 4 miles round trip |
| **Time** | 0.5 to 1 hour |
| **Type** | Loops; out-and-back routes |
| **Elevation Gain/Loss** | Nearly flat |
| **Difficulty** | Moderate |
| **Map** | USGS 7.5-min *San Luis Rey* |
| **Contact** | San Diego County Parks and Recreation Department (858) 694-3049 |

**Trailhead Access**   The Highway 76 expressway east from Interstate 5 makes it easy to reach Guajome Park from the coast. Exit I-5 at Highway 76 and drive east 6 miles to Guajome Lake Rd., past the traffic light at North Santa Fe Dr. There's parking for a fee inside the main entrance, and free roadside parking outside.

**Route Directions**   The westernmost trail in the park skirts a fresh-water marsh that often oozes with moisture even into the dry summer. Flanked by willows and cottonwoods, and overgrown with cattails and volunteer palms, this marshy area exudes a complex mixture of damp odors that you can't often experience in most parts of arid San Diego County.

In the drier and higher eastern part of the park, a combination of dirt roads and narrow trails runs over grassy hill and dale, extending as far as the "Upper Pond," about 1 mile east of the park entrance. Looking beyond the park boundary, you'll note scenery ranging

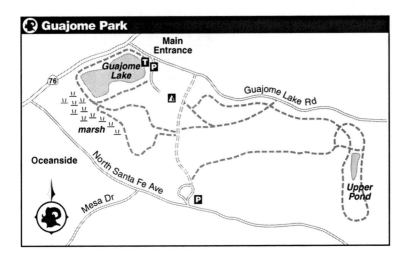

from the sleepy, spacious, semi-rural sprawl of Oceanside's past, to wall-to-wall-style subdivisions that are the wave of the future.

If you piece together a looping route (several are possible) that visits both the marsh and the Upper Pond, you will cover approximately 3 miles in all.

# 29

## DALEY RANCH— MEADOW LOOP

With more than 20 miles of trails for self-propelled travelers, the 3058-acre Daley Ranch, a former cattle spread and dairy north of Escondido, is a runner's paradise. The most runner-friendly route in the park, based on its lack of severe inclines and rough surfaces, is the rambling loop around the edge of Jack Creek Meadow. Runners living or working around Escondido will find this a perfect place to unwind on a spring or summer evening after work.

| | |
|---:|:---|
| **Distance** | 5.6 miles |
| **Time** | 1 to 1.5 hours |
| **Type** | Out and back, with loop |
| **Elevation Gain/Loss** | 500′/500′ |
| **Difficulty** | Moderate |
| **Map** | USGS 7.5-min *Valley Center* |
| **Contact** | Daley Ranch (760) 737-6266 |

**Trailhead Access** From Interstate 15 in Escondido, take El Norte Parkway east 3 miles to La Honda Dr. Turn left on La Honda, following signs to Dixon Lake, and continue 1 mile to the Daley Ranch parking lot (free parking here), right before the Dixon Lake Recreation Area entrance.

**Route Directions** Step around the Daley Ranch gate and immediately get those arms and legs pumping on a vigorous ascent along the paved driveway of the former ranch. At 0.4 mile the road starts descending, and you swoop down into live-oak woods. There you get a glimpse, through a screen of cattails, of one of the largest of several stock ponds on the property. After 1.2 miles pavement ends, and on the left you'll see the quaint redwood Daley ranch house, built in 1928.

Continue north another 200 yards to the beginning of the Jack Creek Meadow Trail. One leg of the trail goes up the east side of the

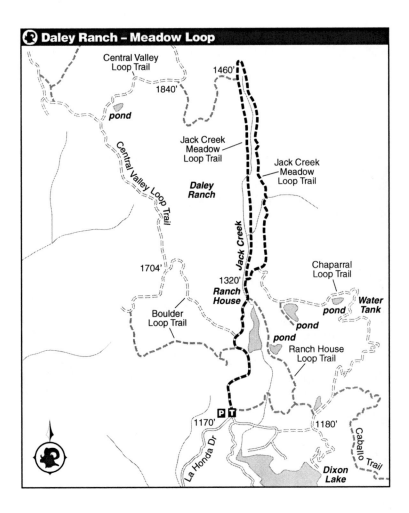

Central Valley
Loop Trail

1460'

1840'

pond

Central Valley Loop Trail

Jack Creek
Meadow
Loop Trail

Jack Creek
Meadow
Loop Trail

Daley
Ranch

Jack Creek

Chaparral
Loop Trail

1704'

1320'
Ranch
House

Water
Tank

pond

Boulder
Loop Trail

pond

pond

Ranch House
Loop Trail

P T
1170'

1180'

Caballo Trail

La Honda Dr

Dixon
Lake

elongated, narrow valley, the other returns on the west side. The meadow, lined with a dark green row of coast live oaks and backed by steep slopes of shaggy chaparral, looks impressive in early-morning or late-afternoon light. Close at hand you pass several gnarled specimens of Engelmann oak, with gray-green leaves and light-colored bark. The meadow grasses are almost entirely nonnative, typically of an emerald green color for about three months in the winter, and bleached yellow-brown after a month or two of springtime sun and prolonged drought. Other than the annoying sight of some powerlines through the meadow, the sense of isolation from the city below is complete.

After finishing the loop around the meadow, return to your car the way you came.

**Trail Notes**  No drinking water is available in Daley Ranch, but there are water faucets in the Dixon Lake Recreation Area.

Along the Jack
Creek Meadow
Loop Trail

# 30

## DALEY RANCH— ENGELMANN LOOP

This northern loop within the Daley Ranch highlights the Engelmann oak (or mesa oak)—a somewhat rare and picturesque evergreen oak tree found only in parts of interior Southern California. Engelmanns, with grayish-green leaves and sparser foliage than other live oaks, tolerate dryness better and tend to thrive on high and low ground. Your route, on rocky fire roads and trails, sticks mostly to that higher ground, which means you'll have panoramic views in various directions.

| | |
|---:|:---|
| **Distance** | 5.1 miles |
| **Time** | 1 to 2 hours |
| **Type** | Out and back, with loop |
| **Elevation Gain/Loss** | 800'/800' |
| **Difficulty** | Moderate |
| **Map** | USGS 7.5-min *Valley Center* |
| **Contact** | Daley Ranch (760) 737-6266 |

**Trailhead Access**

The Engelmann loop route begins at a back entrance to Daley Ranch off the northern extension of Broadway. From Escondido, drive north about 5 miles on Broadway, then follow graded Cougar Pass Rd. 1.4 miles east and north to a gated access road on the right. Limited roadside parking is available.

**Route Directions**

Starting out, you run south across a grassy flat and soon plunge into a thicket of coast live oaks. A small, deeply shaded stream flows here, but only during the rainy season. At 0.7 mile keep straight, ignoring the north segment of the Engelmann Oak Loop Trail, which branches left. At 0.9 mile stay right, avoiding the Bobcat Trail, which will be your return route.

Really climbing now, you soon reach a saddle. Stay on the main road, which angles east, upward along a ridge. You'll encounter a

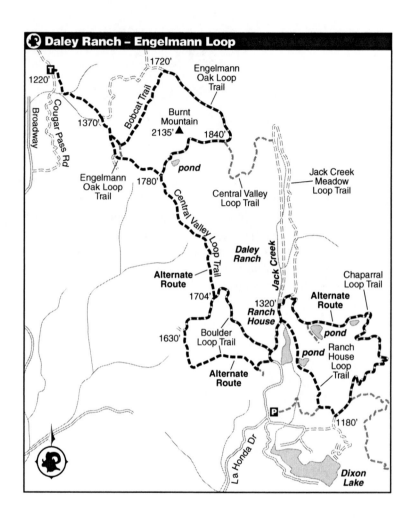

## Daley Ranch – Engelmann Loop

1220' T

Broadway

Cougar Pass Rd

1720'

Engelmann Oak Loop Trail

Bobcat Trail

Burnt Mountain 2135' ▲

1370'

1840'

Engelmann Oak Loop Trail

1780'

pond

Central Valley Loop Trail

Central Valley Loop Trail

Jack Creek Meadow Loop Trail

Daley Ranch

Jack Creek

Alternate Route

1704'

1320' Ranch House

Chaparral Loop Trail

Alternate Route

1630'

Boulder Loop Trail

pond

Ranch House Loop Trail

pond

Alternate Route

P

La Honda Dr

1180'

Dixon Lake

steep section with loose rocks underfoot. Since it's easier to go up this hill than to careen down, this section is the reason for following the loop in the described direction. To take your mind off the intense labor of the climb, gaze down at the spreading suburbs of Escondido.

*A Misnomer*   The English translation of the Spanish word "escondido" is "hidden." The name refers to Escondido's location in an inland valley surrounded by mountains. As you gaze over the cityscape below you can see how out-dated that name is today.

Bear left at the next junction (1.5 miles). Continue climbing, but consider pausing for a rest at the beautiful old stock pond on the right, brimming with water after winter rains. The trail then passes through an agreeable spread of coast live oaks, where your feet intermittently crunch through accumulated oak leaf litter.

You now skirt the south side of Burnt Mountain, a rounded, brushy, boulder-studded promontory that is the high point of the immediate area. At 2.3 miles, stay straight as the Central Valley Loop Trail veers right. As you curve left shortly ahead, there's a view northeast of the rolling mesa occupied by the rural community of Valley Center. You pass a large, blue water tank on the right at 3 miles. Turn left in a grassy vale, 0.3 mile beyond, on the narrow Bobcat Trail. This trail avoids the less-interesting, northern segment of the Engelmann Oak Loop Trail.

Your feet can really fly on the 1-mile descent of the Bobcat Trail. You lose elevation gradually through swaying grass, fragrant chaparral, and finally under densely clustered live oaks whose intertwining limbs nearly blot out the sky. This is surely trail running at its best.

When you reach the next trail fork, bear right, and return to the road you came in on.

**Alternate Routes**

As the map shows, you can piece together more than one running route of 10-plus miles in Daley Ranch. The Chaparral Loop Trail is most agreeable in the winter and spring, when the stock ponds are often full of water. Boulder Loop Trail features jumbo granitic boulders seemingly erupting from the landscape. The Ranch House Loop Trail is practically unrunnable in places due to severe inclines.

**Trail Notes**

No water can be found either at the trailhead or along the route, so take plenty along.

# 31

# BODEN CANYON

Boden Canyon Ecological Reserve is one of San Diego County's newest parcels of protected open space. The 2000-acre reserve lies between Escondido and Ramona, and is yet another link in the unfinished 55-mile-long San Dieguito River Park. With dirt roads and narrower paths featuring gradual ascents and descents, the reserve is ideal for faster-paced workouts amid some of the county's finest foothill landscapes. Mountain bikes, horses, and all forms of motorized transport are prohibited, so there's a chance you'll have the whole place to yourself.

| | |
|---:|:---|
| **Distance** | 11.0 miles round trip |
| **Time** | 1.5 to 2.5 hours |
| **Type** | Out and back |
| **Elevation Gain/Loss** | 500´/500´ |
| **Difficulty** | Moderate |
| **Map** | Boden Canyon map (available at trailhead) |
| **Contact** | California Department of Fish and Game (858) 467-4201 |

**Trailhead Access**  The unmarked trailhead (a dirt-road intersection) is located on the north side of Highway 78, 7 miles east of the San Diego Wild Animal Park and 5 miles west of the Highway 78/67 intersection in Ramona. Park on the dirt road so that you don't block access to other vehicles. Walk downhill, passing a locked vehicle gate. Just beyond is a small bulletin board with a box of maps.

**Route Directions**  From the vehicle gate, descend to a hairpin turn, where the road swings around the bottom of Clevenger Canyon. Sycamores and oaks dot the canyon bottom, with filigrees of poison oak and wild

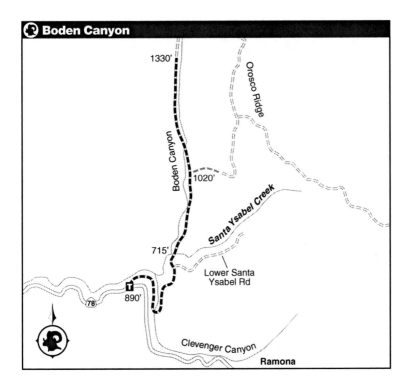

**Boden Canyon**

1330'

Orosco Ridge

Boden Canyon

1020'

Santa Ysabel Creek

715'

Lower Santa
Ysabel Rd

78

890'

Clevenger Canyon

Ramona

grape, giving a small taste of the scenery to come. The little-traveled Lower Santa Ysabel Rd. branches right, and your trail crosses Santa Ysabel Creek (with little or no water in summer and possible torrential flows in winter) on a concrete ford (1.7 miles).

Your course is now almost due north, with little wiggles here and there as you make your way up the wide crease in the landscape known as Boden Canyon. Clusters of live oak trees cast dense pools of shade over the trail at frequent intervals. A few Engelmann oaks and number of fancifully twisted sycamores are here, too. Eucalyptus trees grow in two places, probably at the location of former ranch dwellings. At 5.5 miles into your run, you come to the turnaround point, a locked gate with private land beyond. An old, tumbledown corrugated metal shack hides in the foliage nearby.

Someday, the Boden Canyon route will tie in with the 55-mile Coast to Crest Trail through San Dieguito River Park. At present, there's only one way back, which is the way you came.

**Trail Notes**    No drinking water is available at the trailhead or along the route, though Santa Ysabel Creek may provide cool water for splashing over your body.

**Nature Notes**    The cooler half of the year is unquestionably best for a visit to Boden Canyon. Dozens of varieties of wildflowers pop out in March and April, and a sheen of green covers everything at that time. By June, much of the color fades and the landscape takes on a stern, parched appearance with shades of muted green and brown. The breezy passages through the oak groves are always cool and refreshing any time of year.

The Fish and Game department has established an interim hunting zone in northernmost Boden Canyon, encompassing the last mile of the public path. Be aware that hunting for various game animals may take place in this area during certain seasons.

Oak woodland in
Boden Canyon

# 32

# BLACK MOUNTAIN

Many San Diegans are familiar with the Black Mountain that looms over the Rancho Peñasquitos area near Interstate 15. Farther inland though, 8 miles northeast of Ramona, a much broader and higher—but little-known—mountain with the same name rises to a 4051-foot crest. A fire-lookout tower once stood on "big" Black Mountain's high point, taking full advantage of a unique, panoramic vista furnished by the mountain's strategic central location within San Diego County. The fire-lookout site is the goal for this relentlessly uphill run on fire roads of variable steepness.

| | |
|---|---|
| **Distance** | 14.2 miles round trip (from Pamo Valley) |
| **Time** | 3.5 to 5.5 hours |
| **Type** | Out and back |
| **Elevation Gain/Loss** | 3100′/3100′ |
| **Difficulty** | Strenuous |
| **Map** | USGS 7.5-min *Mesa Grande* |
| **Contact** | Cleveland National Forest, Palomar Ranger District (760) 788-0250 |

**Trailhead Access**

From Highway 67 (Ramona's main drag), go north on 7th Street. Shortly, 7th Street becomes Elm Street. After about 1 mile turn right on Haverford Road, and then immediately left (north) on Pamo Road. Drive north down a steep grade into Pamo Valley and continue 1.3 miles past the end of the pavement to reach a fire road intersecting on the right, Forest Rd. 12S07. We'll assume that you park and start running from here—though it may be possible to drive up the fire road in a 4-wheel-drive or high-clearance vehicle and shorten the out-and-back distance. If you drive up Pamo Rd. as far as Black Mountain Rd. (or farther) and park your vehicle, you will need to display a National Forest Adventure Pass on your car.

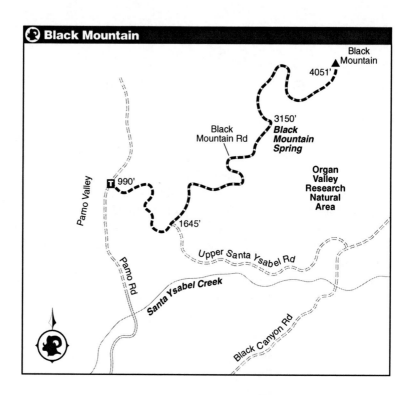

**Black Mountain**

Black Mountain
4051'

3150'
Black
Mountain Rd    **Black
Mountain
Spring**

**Organ
Valley
Research
Natural
Area**

990'

1645'

Pamo Valley

Pamo Rd

*Upper Santa Ysabel Rd*

*Santa Ysabel Creek*

*Black Canyon Rd*

**Route
Directions**    Forest Rd. 12S07 and much of the Black Mountain fire road ahead
are open to travel by car, depending on the season and the condition
of the road. Even so, motorized traffic is slight, and mountain bikes,
hikers, equestrians, and runners usually outnumber cars on the way
to the summit.

    Head uphill (east) from Pamo Road on a steady uphill grade. You
soon cross the boundary of Cleveland National Forest. At 1.5 miles
there's a wide intersection, where the Black Mountain fire road forks
left. Follow the Black Mountain fire road as it curls up the chaparral-
clothed mountainside, heading generally northeast toward the
mountain's broad crest. You can identify the crest from below by a
dark fringe of planted pines growing near the top.

    As you climb, scrubby chamise chaparral gradually yields to sparse
Engelmann oak woodland, and finally to the planted groves of
Coulter pines and other drought-resistant coniferous trees near the
top. The Organ Valley Research Natural Area, a square mile of oak-
dotted ravines and slopes designated for special protection, lies east of

Running the
Black Mountain
fire road

the road. You may notice a hiker's entryway into this natural area 4.8
miles up from Pamo Rd. At 5.3 miles you pass a perennial spring and
fire-fighting reservoir on the right, where horses and dogs can fill
their bellies with cool, slightly murky water.

The road ends at 6.9 miles. On a very rough, 0.2 mile final stretch
along a bulldozed former roadway—almost certainly at a hiking and
not a running pace—you can reach the fire-tower site. Concrete
steps, footings, and a cistern remain, amid a purple-flowering carpet
of nonnative vinca, or periwinkle. Using fingers and toes you can
boost yourself atop the concrete cistern. There you can swing your
head around for a 360-degree panorama not available anywhere else
in San Diego County. In the near distance north and east, you're
looking down on the rolling pasturelands of Mesa Grande, a hidden
landscape famous in geology circles for its deposits of the mineral
tourmaline. To the west, the cobalt-blue or sparkling silver ocean
reveals itself on the clearest days. In every other direction, range after
range of rounded mountains march out to the horizon.

Return the same way, taking care not to injure your knees on the
7-mile descent.

**Trail Notes**

The nearest available drinking water is in Ramona. Fill up before
you drive out to Pamo Valley.

**Nature Notes**

Unquestionably, late fall through early winter is the perfect time to
enjoy this trek. Excellent visibility is common then due to the cool,

dry air. In March and April the dominant chaparral vegetation is dressed up in its best spring-green foliage—though by April the skies are often a bit dewy with coastal haze.

# THE MOUNTAINS

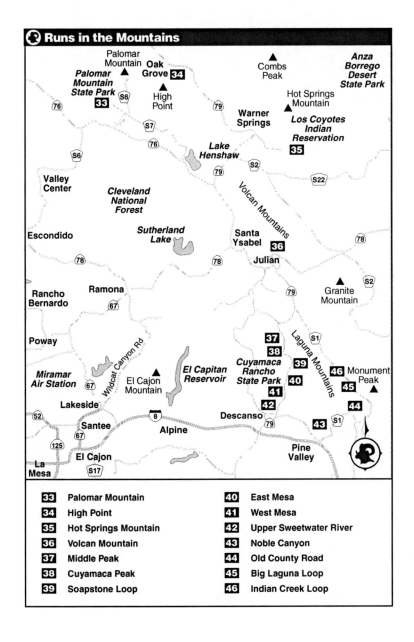

**Runs in the Mountains**

| | | | |
|---|---|---|---|
| **33** | Palomar Mountain | **40** | East Mesa |
| **34** | High Point | **41** | West Mesa |
| **35** | Hot Springs Mountain | **42** | Upper Sweetwater River |
| **36** | Volcan Mountain | **43** | Noble Canyon |
| **37** | Middle Peak | **44** | Old County Road |
| **38** | Cuyamaca Peak | **45** | Big Laguna Loop |
| **39** | Soapstone Loop | **46** | Indian Creek Loop |

# 33

## PALOMAR MOUNTAIN

This grand tour of the 1700-acre Palomar Mountain State Park takes you over forested hill and through grassy dale, in a landscape you might suppose belongs to the lushly forested foothills of the Sierra Nevada rather than "dry" Southern California. The nearly 40 inches of average annual rainfall that Palomar receives (three or four times that of coastal San Diego) supports thick forests of oak, pine, cedar, and fir. It also feeds several small streams that lace the park's valleys. With this route's constantly changing scenery, you'll never be bored!

|  |  |
|---:|:---|
| **Distance** | 6.7 miles |
| **Time** | 1.5 to 2.5 hours |
| **Type** | Loop |
| **Elevation Gain/Loss** | 1100′/1100′ |
| **Difficulty** | Moderate |
| **Map** | Palomar Mountain State Park map/brochure (available on entry) |
| **Contact** | Palomar Mountain State Park (760) 742-3462 |

**Trailhead Access**

From eastern Escondido, drive up County Highway S-6 (Valley Parkway and then Valley Center Rd.) up through the community of Valley Center and then down to a T-intersection with State Highway 76. Go 5 miles east on Highway 76 to South Grade Rd., on the left. Endlessly winding South Grade Rd. takes you to the main crossroads atop Palomar Mountain—the intersection of East Grade Rd. and South Grade Rd. Make two left turns in quick succession to point your car west on East Grade Rd. After 3 miles you'll reach the entrance to Palomar Mountain State Park (a day-use fee is due here). Park at Silver Crest Picnic Area, just beyond the entrance.

Opposite page: Doane Pond, Palomar Mountain State Park

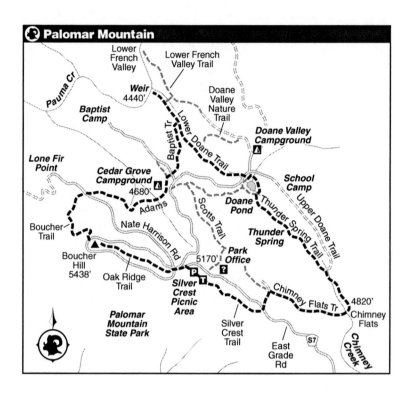

**Palomar Mountain**

Lower French Valley

Lower French Valley Trail

Pauma Cr

Weir 4440'

Doane Valley Nature Trail

Baptist Camp

Baptist Tr

Lower Doane Trail

Doane Valley Campground

Lone Fir Point

Cedar Grove Campground 4680'

Adams

Scotts Trail

Doane Pond

Thunder Spring Trail

Upper Doane Trail

School Camp

Boucher Trail

Nate Harrison Rd

Thunder Spring

Boucher Hill 5438'

Oak Ridge Trail

Park Office 5170'

Silver Crest Picnic Area

Chimney Flats Tr

4820' Chimney Flats

Palomar Mountain State Park

Silver Crest Trail

East Grade Rd

S7

Chimney Creek

---

From the picnic area where you parked, return to the paved entrance road and jog farther west for a couple of minutes to a junction where five narrow roads, including the one you are on, come together. In between the two roads on the left (both forming a loop that encircles Boucher Hill) follow the narrow Oak Ridge Trail uphill along the crest of a rounded ridge. Deciduous black oaks cling to this ridgeline, their limbs bare in winter but covered with shimmering golden leaves in October and November. A few Christmas-tree-like white firs appear as you approach the antenna facility on Boucher Hill, 1.0 mile from the start.

A viewpoint on the west brow of Boucher Hill offers an expansive view west down to Pauma Valley and dry foothills below, and infrequently out to as far as the Pacific Ocean.

Now find the Boucher Trail, which descends the slope to the north. Beyond more black oaks, bracken ferns, and patches of meadow, the trail swings right to traverse a north slope and enters a dense, almost gloomy forest of white fir. Cross Nate Harrison Rd. and pick up the Adams Trail on the other side. You're in mixed forest now, strongly reminiscent of the west-side Sierra Nevada woodland. Winding around a sunlight-flooded ravine, you'll see beautiful specimens of dogwood and wild lilac, in bloom during April and May. In early summer, yellow Humboldt lilies unfold their petals in shady areas.

When you reach Cedar Grove Campground, 2.1 miles, swing left around the campsites to connect with the Baptist Trail. Climb up and over a small rise (crossing a paved access road) and descend sharply into a picture-postcard-perfect Lower Doane Valley. At 2.8 miles, you connect with the streamside Lower Doane Trail in Lower Doane Valley. Turn left and follow Lower Doane Trail for a quarter of a mile over to a picturesque old weir on Pauma Creek. The 1920s-vintage stone-and-mortar dam and gauging station were used to test the hydroelectric potential of the creek, which it turns out was too weak to justify even a small powerplant installation. This is a perfectly serene spot for resting and dipping your feet in the cool, shallow water, if you're inclined.

From the weir, retrace your steps to the Baptist Trail junction, and continue following the Lower Doane Trail up along the valley's edge—with Doane Creek on the left, its silvery surface reflecting the screen of riparian vegetation thriving along its banks.

At 4.1 miles you reach the parking lot adjacent to Doane Pond (drinking water is available here). Swing around this small fishing pond left or right, and continue, again moderately uphill, along the Thunder Spring Trail, which traces the west margin of Upper Doane Valley. A side path on the right leads to a shady ravine where giant chain ferns frame Thunder Spring.

At the south end of the valley, 5.0 miles, veer right and commence a brief, heart-pounding climb on a rough trail up the drainage of Chimney Creek. Native azalea grows thickly in here, displaying white blossoms in mid-spring. At the top of the steepest part, you emerge in Chimney Flats, an oak-fringed meadow dotted with bracken ferns. You then bear right (west) on the Chimney Flats Trail, which follows an old fire road. Climb more moderately now through the forest to another flat (6.0 miles), this one filled with the remains of an apple orchard planted more than a century ago. Beyond, turn left onto a service road and follow it across nearby East Grade Rd. On the far side pick up the Silver Crest Trail which will take you the remaining half mile back to your starting point, Silver Crest Picnic Area.

**Trail Notes**   Water is available at the trailhead, and about two thirds of the way around the loop at Doane Pond.

**Nature Notes**   In San Diego County, poison oak grows from sea level to about 4500 feet elevation, although in the case of Palomar Mountain State Park, it flourishes at elevations somewhat higher than that. Keep an eye out for it around oak trees. Also avoid brushing against any twigs encroaching upon the trail; the barren twigs of poison oak contain the same skin-irritating oil found in the leaves.

# 34

# HIGH POINT

How's this for a grunt and a groan: Climb Palomar Mountain from base to top, starting at Oak Grove on the east side and ending at the 6140-foot summit named High Point? High Point is the highest Palomar summit, and also tops all other summits within a radius of 14 miles, so you're almost guaranteed a good view.

| | |
|---|---|
| **Distance** | 13.0 miles round trip |
| **Time** | 3.5 to 5.5 hours |
| **Type** | Out and back |
| **Elevation Gain/Loss** | 3600′/3600′ |
| **Difficulty** | Strenuous |
| **Map** | USGS 7.5-min *Aguanga, Palomar Observatory* |
| **Contact** | Cleveland National Forest, Palomar Ranger District (760) 788-0250 |

**Trailhead Access**

Oak Grove, a tiny backcountry community near the Riverside County line, lies 14 miles north of Warner Springs and 24 miles east of Temecula by way of Highway 79. Begin at the fire station at mile 49.1 on Highway 79, just west of the highway.

**Route Directions**

Follow the OAK GROVE TRAIL signs directing you over dirt roads and footpaths behind the station. After crossing a small stream just behind the station, the trail meanders up to a ridgeline and begins cutting back and forth across an old firebreak. Only the strongest runners will maintain their running stride on this fiercely steep pitch.

You make your way up through wiry growths of chamise, ribbonwood, scrub oak, and manzanita, all the while gaining better perspectives of the lower hills and valleys below. Springtime growths of annual wildflowers brighten the scene nearby. If it's clear enough, the

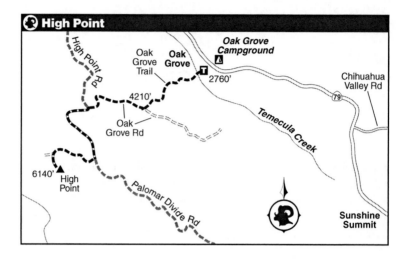

view to the north starts to include the sometimes snowy summits of San Gorgonio Mountain and San Jacinto Peak.

At 1.8 miles and 1450 feet higher, you reach graded Oak Grove Rd. Turn right and continue uphill on a mercifully more gradual grade toward an intersection with High Point Rd. at 3.4 miles. Turn left and continue gaining elevation through chaparral and oak forest until you reach Palomar Divide Rd., 5.2 miles. Go right there, and travel west around the north flank of High Point through a cool, shady forest of oaks and pines. At 6.2 miles you veer left on the steep road to the summit.

---

*Palomar Fire Tower*    The 67-foot-high fire tower on the summit is one of the remaining few in San Diego County in reasonable repair. You may be able to climb up the first few flights of steps for a better view of the surroundings. The list of peaks visible—including the one you're on—reads like a roster of the highest points in Southern California. Combs Peak, whose summit is right about eye level if you stand on the tower, is the nearest rival, 14 miles to the east. Parts of the Santa Rosa, San Ysidro, and Vallecito mountains in the Anza-Borrego Desert are visible, along with the Laguna and Cuyamaca mountains farther to the southeast. In the north are the real giants—Old Baldy, San Gorgonio, and San Jacinto. On very clear days, several of the Channel Islands are visible far out in the Pacific. A lookout here once reported a fire burning in Santa Barbara County, almost 200 miles away.

---

Storm clouds
gathering in
the Palomar
Mountains

The High Point summit area can be approached by way of High **Alternate**
Point Rd. from Highway 79 at Aguanga (11 miles of dirt road); and **Routes**
by way of Palomar Divide Rd. from a point on Highway 79 south of
Sunshine Summit (12 miles of dirt road). These fire roads are seasonally open for high-clearance vehicles, and offer methods of
approaching High Point more closely before you get out and run.
Oak Grove Rd., however, is closed to public travel at its lower end.

No water is available en route, and shade is hard to come by on the **Trail Notes**
lower two-thirds of the route, which climbs the drier, hotter eastern
slope of Palomar. Plan accordingly!

# 35

# HOT SPRINGS MOUNTAIN

Some of the loftiest—and loneliest—mountain country in San Diego County lies on the 25,000-acre Los Coyotes Indian Reservation. You won't find any casino here, but you will discover San Diego County's obscure high point, Hot Springs Mountain. At elevation 6533 feet it beats the better-known, 6512-foot Cuyamaca Peak by a whisker. The reservation welcomes weekend visitors for camping, hiking, running, mountain biking, and off-road vehicle driving. A ban on trail motorcycles keeps the place reasonably quiet and free of flying dust. Wait till you see the view—it's ethereal.

|  |  |
|---:|:---|
| **Distance** | 15.2 miles round trip |
| **Time** | 4 to 6 hours |
| **Type** | Out and back |
| **Elevation Gain/Loss** | 2900´/2900´ |
| **Difficulty** | Strenuous |
| **Map** | USGS 7.5-min *Hot Springs Mtn.* |
| **Contact** | Los Coyotes Indian Reservation (760) 782-0711 |

**Trailhead Access**  Turn east on Camino San Ignacio from Highway 79 (mile 35.0) at Warner Springs. After 0.6 mile, bear right and continue 4.5 miles to the reservation gate. There you pay a $10-per-car fee and can pick up a sketch map of the reservation's roads and trails.

**Route Directions**  Hot Springs Mountain may be reached by way of three distinct routes, the longest of which, described here, offers the most gradual and view-rich approach. Remember, you'll be sharing the road with high-clearance motorized vehicles, and with your own vehicle of this type you could short-cut this running route to any degree you wish. We'll assume that you begin 0.2 mile up the road from the

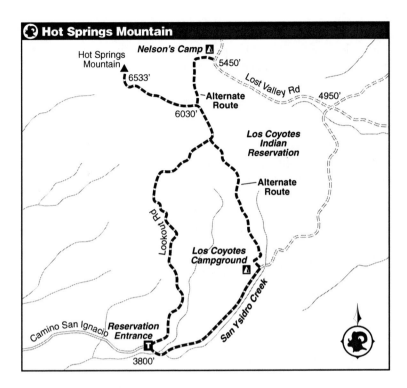

Hot Springs Mountain

6533'

Nelson's Camp

5450'

Lost Valley Rd

4950'

Alternate Route

6030'

Los Coyotes Indian Reservation

Alternate Route

Lookout Rd

Los Coyotes Campground

San Ysidro Creek

Camino San Ignacio

Reservation Entrance

3800'

entry gate, where Lookout Rd. splits left. You face a 7.6-mile climb by starting at this junction, following Lookout Rd. all the way.

With an early enough start, the somewhat desolate, scrubby landscape traversed by the lower part of Lookout Rd. looks reasonably inviting. By about 2 miles the steepness of the constantly curving road eases a bit, and soon you enter a more agreeable-looking landscape of thicker chaparral and protruding granitic outcrops.

The view south and west keeps improving, until it culminates at 4.0 miles as the road curves to the right around the shoulder of a ridge. You now have a broad vista southwest of the rolling grasslands of Valle de San Jose and the reservoir it harbors—Lake Henshaw— and find yourself on cool, forested, north-facing slopes, enjoying a delightful 1-plus mile passage with little elevation gain. The largest and most statuesque trees growing here are sugar pines, with wandlike limbs and long, narrow cones.

At 5.4 miles a lesser dirt road originating at the Los Coyotes Campground joins from the right, and at 6.0 miles another road on the right (more of a wide trail, but labeled "dangerous road" on the

Los Coyotes reservation sketch map) begins a steep dive down the north slope of the mountain. You now stick to a road heading northwest along a gently rolling, lightly wooded ridge, with small ups and downs, before tackling the final 200-foot climb to the top of the road, 7.6 miles from your starting point.

| | |
|---|---|
| *Getting the* *Best View* | Just west of the road summit stands a rickety old fire lookout tower, disused since 1976, with rotting and broken wooden steps. A better view awaits you just east, on a flat concrete platform topping a large boulder. A bit of hand-and-toe climbing is required to gain the last 20 feet of elevation. This is the true summit of Hot Springs Mountain, where you'll have a view of steep canyons yawning to the west and north and the Salton Sea shimmering like a mirage on the eastern horizon. On sunny days, soaring enthusiasts ride the thermals and quietly buzz the summit in their lean-looking aircraft. |

**Alternate Routes** The steep, rough jeep trail ascending from the Los Coyotes Campground to mile 5.4 on the Lookout Rd. can be used on the ascending or descending lower leg of the climb—instead of the main Lookout Rd.

The most direct route by foot, though, is the short and very steep climb up from Nelson's Camp, a remote campsite in the north part of the reservation. On that route you hook up with Lookout Rd. at

At the true
summit, Hot
Springs Mountain

its 6.0-mile mark, and then use Lookout Rd. to reach the top of the mountain. That out-and-back run measures 5.6 miles round trip, with elevation gains and losses of 1250 feet. Some 20 or 30 minutes of extra driving one-way is required to reach Nelson's Camp.

**Trail Notes** Bring cash to pay the entry fee, which is currently $10 per car. Attendants are not always on duty, especially in the early morning. You can pick up a sketch map of the reservation at the entrance, but the USGS topographic map is much better at showing the details of the route you will be on.

**Nature Notes** Although the Los Coyotes Indian Reservation primarily welcomes weekend visitors, it may be possible to run here during the week— and have most of 25,000 acres of nearly deserted open space available to you—if you call ahead first and try to make arrangements.

# 36

# VOLCAN MOUNTAIN

Volcan Mountain (also known as the Volcan Mountains) near Julian is the most exciting example of prime mountain landscape being added to the county's roster of public lands. The county and other agencies are purchasing some 10,000-plus acres of a former private ranch for eventual inclusion into the county park system and into the 55-mile-long linear park known as the San Dieguito River Park. Well over half of this total acreage has already been deeded to public agencies—but only one section of 800 acres, the Volcan Mountain Preserve, with a single steep trail going part way up the mountain, has been opened to the public so far. Eventually, when the mountain's view-rich crest, its forested valleys, and its plunging ravines are fully accessible, this will be a superb, spacious place to explore for hours at a time.

| | |
|---:|:---|
| **Distance** | 3.2 miles round trip (to gate) |
| **Time** | 1 to 1.5 hours |
| **Type** | Out and back |
| **Elevation Gain/Loss** | 800´/800´ |
| **Difficulty** | Moderate |
| **Map** | USGS 7.5-min *Julian* |
| **Contact** | San Diego County Parks and Recreation Department (858) 694-3049 |

**Trailhead Access**  On Farmer Rd., northbound out of Julian, drive 2 miles to Wynola Rd. Make a brief jog right, then left, remaining on Farmer Rd. Park along Farmer Rd., 200 yards north of Wynola Rd., where a dirt road strikes off to the right (east).

**Route Directions**  Don't drive on the dirt road; it's for public access to the preserve on foot only. You pass by apple orchards (Julian's signature crop) and at

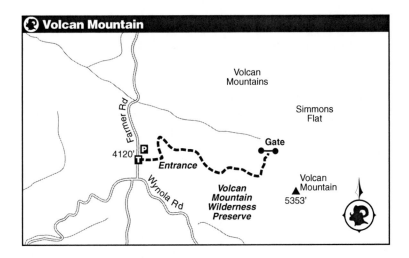

0.2 mile arrive at a carved entrance gate for the preserve. The entry, and a nearby open-air, stonework *kiva* (used for interpretive programs) were designed by noted Julian artist James Hubbell. The Elsinore Fault, a major splinter of the San Andreas, passes almost directly under this spot.

On a less distinct road—gradually becoming a mere trail—you swing north, round a horseshoe bend, and pant in earnest as you climb along a rounded ridgeline leading toward Volcan peak. Along the ridge, wind-rippled expanses of grassland alternate with dense copses of live oak, and the view expands to include the townsite of Julian, its "suburb" of Whispering Pines, and the dusky Cuyamaca Mountains to the south.

At 1.4 miles beyond the Volcan Mountain Preserve entryway, you come to a locked gate. Before heading back, enjoy watching birds of prey soaring over the grassy slopes hereabouts, and admire the view in the northwest of rolling hills and wooded hollows on the upper Santa Ysabel Creek drainage.

**Alternate Routes**

Perhaps soon (pending completion of a county management plan for the area) it will be possible to proceed all the way to so-called Volcan peak, the southernmost of several knolls along the crest of the range. You can visit that area now, but only by participating in one of the hikes led by San Diego County Parks rangers or docents.

**Trail Notes**  No water is available either at the trailhead or along the route. Parts of the route are very steep; watch your footing on the downhill return.

**Nature Notes**  Much of the east slope of Volcan Mountain was thoroughly charred by the 2002 Pines Fire, but the blaze consumed mostly chaparral vegetation and not much of the richly forested areas covering parts of the summit ridge.

In October 2003, fire once again ate its way into western sections of the Volcan Mountains, but not this area. During the Cedar Fire (see p. 140), a monumental effort by firefighters saved the historic town of Julian, and prevented the blaze from spreading into Volcan Mountain Wilderness Preserve.

During the next several winter and spring seasons, the burned areas should come to life with the growth of fresh green grass and fire-following wildflowers.

Entrance,
Volcan Mountain
Preserve

# 37

# MIDDLE PEAK

This is what mountain running is all about! With its nearly 30,000 acres of forests, meadows, and chaparral-covered slopes, Cuyamaca Rancho State Park is the crown jewel of San Diego County's mountain landscapes. Middle Peak is the best of the best—as long as you appreciate wooded mountainsides and fern glades.

| | |
|---|---|
| **Distance** | 5.7 miles |
| **Time** | 1.5 to 2.5 hours |
| **Type** | Loop |
| **Elevation Gain/Loss** | 1100′ / 1100′ |
| **Difficulty** | Moderately strenuous |
| **Map** | Cuyamaca Rancho State Park map/brochure, available at the park's campgrounds and headquarters. USGS 7.5-min *Cuyamaca Peak* shows the topography better. |
| **Contact** | Cuyamaca Rancho State Park (760) 765-0755 |

**Trailhead Access**

Begin at the roadside parking area and major trailhead just south of Cuyamaca Reservoir, mile 10.7 on Highway 79. This is 10.7 miles north of Old Highway 80 near Descanso, and 9 miles south of Julian.

**Route Directions**

From the trailhead go west across Highway 79 and jog north along the narrow Minshall Trail, which parallels the nearly flat roadway. At about 0.7 mile, you diverge a bit from the highway, veer left behind several cabins, and join a dirt road. Continue 0.2 mile on that dirt road, then go left on the marked Sugar Pine Trail, a former fire road.

Now you face nearly 2 miles of climbing at a moderate grade—made a bit more difficult due to the thinner air at this roughly mile-high elevation.

In the late afternoon of October 25, 2003, a small wildfire ignited in a remote part of the Cleveland National Forest, near Cedar Creek, several miles west of Middle Peak. By midnight the flames—driven by Santa Ana winds from the northeast—were racing southwest toward the northern and eastern suburbs of San Diego, some 25 miles away. By the following day, the Cedar Fire (as it was known by then) was burning hundreds of homes on the edge of the city. One day later, the winds reversed, and the Cedar Fire began to spread east and northeast toward Julian and the crest of the Cuyamaca Mountains. Nearly all of Cuyamaca Rancho State Park burned on October 29 and 30. By October 31, a total of 280,000 acres had been consumed. The Cedar Fire entered the record books as the largest single fire in California history.

From the perspectives of natural resources and recreation, Cuyamaca Rancho State Park was the most heavily damaged of all the wilderness and recreation areas in the Cedar Fire's path. Facilities, such as the park's historic headquarters and the Los Caballos horse camp, were destroyed—though other camp and picnic facilities survived intact or partially damaged. Islands of forest remained here and there, singed but probably not killed by the flames.

At the time of writing, Cuyamaca Rancho State Park was closed to all entry, and was expected to open sometime in spring 2004. Travelers into the burned area were warned to stay on existing trails so as to minimize erosion and allow seeds to germinate on the ash-covered slopes.

Black Oaks
in spring,
Middle Peak

The recovery of meadows and chaparral-covered landscapes will likely take only a few years, while the fate of the formerly dense forest remains to be seen. Some unburned trees will doubtless thrive, while others may not. Coniferous forests may naturally be replaced by oak woodland or chaparral, depending on the amount of precipitation over the next decade or two. There may be tree planting efforts. Experts have agreed that the Cuyamaca landscape will not look the same again for many decades to come.

Visitors to the park can expect to see fascinating changes over the next several seasons, as fire-following wildflowers bloom in the spring and plants and animals slowly and surely return.

---

At 2.5 miles the road passes the foundation of an old cabin and then curves southwest to join Middle Peak Fire Rd. Keep left at the intersection, go 50 yards, and then turn left, staying on Middle Peak Fire Rd. heading east. The 5883-foot summit of Middle Peak now lies south and about 200 feet above you.

Run east and later south (downhill all the way). Stay to the right to join the Black Oak Trail as Middle Peak Fire Rd. veers left (or east). After an easy-going short mile on the Black Oak Trail, you'll arrive at a 5-way intersection of roads and trails on the saddle between Middle and Cuyamaca peaks. Make a hard left on Milk Ranch Rd. to begin the last leg of the run. The remaining 1.7 miles on graded dirt road are gradually downhill.

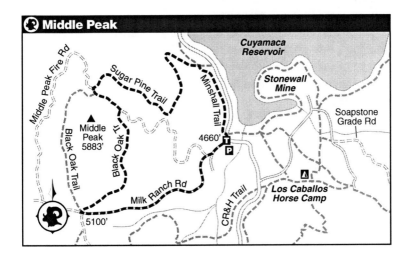

*Trees of the*    The Sugar Pine Trail owes its name to the magnificent growths of sugar
*Trail*    pines along the trail's upper end. You'll recognize this species of pine by its long, narrow cones on the tips of drooping branches, and the "puzzle patterns" in its peeling bark. Outside of Palomar Mountain State Park, this north-slope area of Middle Peak harbors probably the most heterogeneous forest in San Diego County. Plenty of black oaks, live oaks, white firs, incense cedars, and ponderosa pines add to the mix.

**Alternate Routes**    As the Middle Peak map shows, there are various ways to circle Middle Peak, using various fire roads and trails. Any or all can be used to extend your workout. Middle Peak Fire Rd., along the peak's semi-forested lower west slope is offers occasional glimpses of Cuyamaca's western foothills, the coastal plain, and at best the Pacific Ocean.

**Trail Notes**    No drinking water is available at the trailhead and none can be found en route.

**Nature Notes**    On warm summer days, pesky gnats can detract from the Middle Peak experience. This problem is minimized during dry years—or else you can run here during the cool of the morning.

April and early May are often crisp, with plenty of bright green color in the black oak's newly emerging leaves. Late October through November brings peak autumn color, crisp, clear mornings, and sometimes warm afternoons.

Sightings of mountain lions at Cuyamaca Rancho State Park have become more common over the last decade. Normally secretive, these creatures have exhibited threatening behavior toward park visitors—hikers, runners, mountain bikers, and equestrians alike. It is recommended that you do not run alone in the park. For further information about dealing with mountain lions, see page 11 in the introduction to this book.

# 38

# CUYAMACA PEAK

Cuyamaca Peak, number two on San Diego County's roster of high points, lies close to the county's geographic center. The paved but closed-to-traffic Lookout Rd. is the most direct route to the Cuyamaca's summit from the highway below. Consider this clear-day scenario: After one hour of driving and one hour of uphill running, you could be gazing down on San Diego Bay or coastal San Diego, having started your journey down there only two hours before.

A fire-lookout tower stood on the Cuyamaca summit until the 1980s, when it was replaced by a small complex of telecommunications antennas. Because of that change, the view isn't as comprehensively panoramic as it could be—but spectacular, nonetheless.

| | |
|---:|---|
| **Distance** | 5.5 miles round trip |
| **Time** | 1.5 to 2.5 hours |
| **Type** | Out and back |
| **Elevation Gain/Loss** | 1650′ / 1650′ |
| **Difficulty** | Moderately strenuous |
| **Map** | Cuyamaca Rancho State Park map/brochure, available at the park's campgrounds and headquarters. USGS 7.5-min *Cuyamaca Peak* shows the topography better. |
| **Contact** | Cuyamaca Rancho State Park (760) 765-0755 |

**Trailhead Access**

Begin at Paso Picacho Campground/Picnic Area, which lies on the west side of Highway 79, 9 miles north of Old Highway 80 near Descanso, and 11 miles south of Julian. The turnoff for Paso Picacho is exactly where Highway 79 summits at an elevation of 4870 feet. Day-use parking is available, for a small fee, next to the picnic sites.

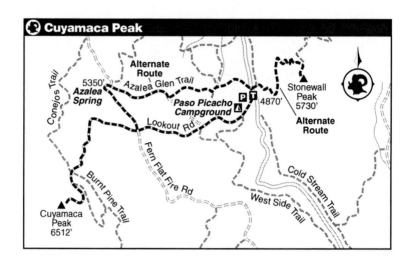

**Cuyamaca Peak**

Alternate Route
Conejos Trail
5350' Azalea Spring
Azalea Glen Trail
Paso Picacho Campground
Lookout Rd
4870'
Stonewall Peak 5730'
Alternate Route
Fern Flat Fire Rd
Burnt Pine Trail
Cuyamaca Peak 6512'
West Side Trail
Cold Stream Trail

**Route Directions**

Lookout Rd. intersects Highway 79 just south of the Paso Picacho entrance. You can also reach the lowermost end of this road from Paso Picacho's southernmost campsites. Whichever way you hook up with it, you will find the initial grade up through pint-sized oaks and pines to be only moderately steep—though it might feel more difficult due to the thinner air at this altitude.

After you cross the California Riding and Hiking Trail at 1.2 miles, (called Fern Flat Fire Rd. to the south and Azalea Spring Fire Rd. to the north), the paved road gets seriously steep, and remains so for the rest of the run. Only the most fit of runners will be able to maintain a jogging stride for the remaining climb.

Views improve as you swing around a sharp left curve (1.7 miles). The vista to the north and east includes Cuyamaca Reservoir and dark-colored mountain ranges within the Anza-Borrego Desert State Park.

At 2.3 miles you arrive at a sunny saddle, where the Conejos Trail intersects and the road momentarily flattens out. Then there's another steep ascent up Cuyamaca's east slope that ends, suddenly, at the antenna facility on the summit.

On the return to Paso Picacho you can really fly—and do so reasonably safely. Such is the advantage of smooth pavement, as opposed to a rough or rocky trail surface.

**Five-County View**

During the clearest weather, the view from Cuyamaca Peak stretches into at least five counties and into northern Baja California. The Pacific Ocean

Cuyamaca Peak

sometimes appears in the west or southwest, more often made visible by
the shimmering reflection of the afternoon sun on its surface than by its
blue tint.

---

Returning by way of the Azalea Glen Trail is rewarding if you don't **Alternate**
mind taking a little extra time. The south portion of that loop trail is **Routes**
better for running—wider and smoother—than the narrow and
steeper north portion. Conejos Trail, as an alternate descent route, is
more trouble than it's worth. Years of erosion in the decomposed
granite soil have created deep furrows, and the trail is full of jagged
rocks.

   If it's smoother, unpaved trail surfaces you desire, however, consider the climb from Paso Picacho to the top of Stonewall Peak, 4.5
miles round trip with a gain and loss of 850 feet. This being the most
popular single trail in Cuyamaca, you'll want to be extra courteous
when passing hikers and especially small children.

Drinking water is available only at the trailhead. The paved road is **Trail Notes**
smooth, but very steep in its upper reaches.

Sightings of mountain lions at Cuyamaca Rancho State Park have **Nature Notes**
become more common over the last decade. Normally secretive,
these creatures have exhibited threatening behavior toward park visitors—hikers, runners, mountain bikers, and equestrians alike. It is

recommended that you do not run alone in the park. For further information about dealing with mountain lions, see page 11 in the introduction to this book.

At press time, the October 2003 Cedar Fire had recently swept across the entire Cuyamaca Rancho State Park, profoundly altering its appearance (see p. 140).

# 39

# SOAPSTONE LOOP

Flat ground is hard to come by in mountainous Cuyamaca Rancho State Park, with the exception of this easy-going, looping route through the headwaters of the Sweetwater River. It's hardly flat, mind you, but at least gentle ascents and descents are the rule most of the way. The route visits the gentle valleys of Stonewall Creek and the upper Sweetwater River (known as Upper Green Valley). A riparian strip of oaks, pines, and willows provides an agreeable accompaniment much of the way, and your chances of sighting deer, coyotes, and other wildlife are very good.

| | |
|---|---|
| **Distance** | 8.2 miles |
| **Time** | 1.5 to 2.5 hours |
| **Type** | Loop |
| **Elevation Gain/Loss** | 1050′/1050′ |
| **Difficulty** | Moderate |
| **Map** | Cuyamaca Rancho State Park map/brochure, available at the park's campgrounds and headquarters. USGS 7.5-min *Cuyamaca Peak* shows the topography better. |
| **Contact** | Cuyamaca Rancho State Park (760) 765-0755 |

**Trailhead Access**

Begin at the small trailhead parking lot on the east side of Highway 79 at mile 7.3. This is 7.3 miles north of Old Highway 80 near Descanso, and about 13 miles south of Julian.

**Route Directions**

Start by crossing the creek behind the parking area and go east about 100 feet to join the Cold Stream Trail. Go left (north) and continue about 200 yards to Cold Spring. From there, bear right on the Cold Spring Trail and follow it northeast 1.2 miles, up through oaks and

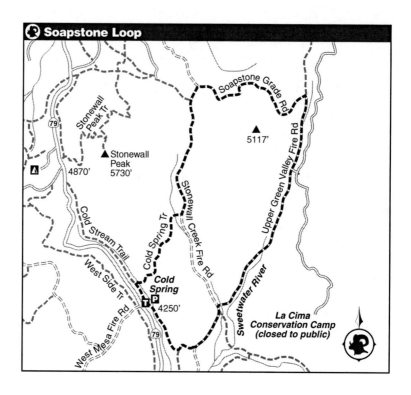

**Soapstone Loop**

chaparral for about 250 feet of gain, and down for a loss of about 200 feet. You'll then cross Stonewall Creek—dry in summer and fall, trickling or bubbling otherwise. Turn left (north) when you reach Stonewall Creek Fire Rd. on the far bank of the creek.

Now you commence a gradual ascent alongside the creek, passing through chaparral, oaks, and pines, and finally across grassland, to a low saddle.

Just beyond the low saddle, you arrive at Soapstone Grade Rd. Turn right (east) and skirt the edge of the broad, open valley containing Cuyamaca Reservoir. The road is named after the soft rock called soapstone, samples of which can be seen underfoot here and there on the road's rocky surface.

After maintaining a near level course for about a mile on Soapstone Grade Rd., you descend sharply for about three quarters of a mile and meet the Upper Green Valley Fire Rd. amid a canopy of spreading oaks. You'll turn right there (south) and cruise easily for the next 2.7 miles as you descend very gradually 2.3 miles to a junction with Stonewall Creek Fire Rd. and continue 0.4 mile to a narrow cutoff trail on the right. Go west on that trail for another 0.4 mile, passing over a low ridge. You then merge into northbound Cold Stream Trail, and in just 0.6 mile you'll be back at your starting point.

Sightings of mountain lions at Cuyamaca Rancho State Park have **Nature Notes** become more common over the last decade. Normally secretive, these creatures have exhibited threatening behavior toward park visitors—hikers, runners, mountain bikers, and equestrians alike. It is recommended that you do not run alone in the park. For further information about dealing with mountain lions, see page 11 in the introduction to this book.

At press time, the October 2003 Cedar Fire had recently swept across the entire Cuyamaca Rancho State Park, profoundly altering its appearance (see p. 140).

# 40

# EAST MESA

Tracing a rough circle around the eastern side of Cuyamaca Rancho State Park, the East Mesa loop follows the Harvey Moore equestrian trail up and over the rolling meadows of East Mesa and down the narrow canyon of Harper Creek. There's plenty of scenic variety along the way, and the nearly constant elevation change keeps your mind and body engaged in the agony and the ecstasy of the journey. East Mesa is Cuyamaca's most wildlife-rich zone, with common sightings of mule deer and coyotes, and less common glimpses of bobcats, mountain lions, skunks, and rabbits.

| | |
|---:|:---|
| **Distance** | 10.5 miles |
| **Time** | 2 to 3 hours |
| **Type** | Loop |
| **Elevation Gain/Loss** | 1300´/1300´ |
| **Difficulty** | Moderately strenuous |
| **Map** | Cuyamaca Rancho State Park map/brochure, available at the park's campgrounds and headquarters. USGS 7.5-min *Cuyamaca Peak* shows the topography better. |
| **Contact** | Cuyamaca Rancho State Park (760) 765-0755 |

**Trailhead Access**  The trailhead for the Harvey Moore Trail is the Sweetwater River bridge parking area, between mile 4.8 and 4.9 on Highway 79. This is 4.8 miles north of Old Highway 80 near Descanso, and 15 miles south of Julian.

**Route Directions**  From the trailhead, follow the Harvey Moore Trail south and east across a hillside, passing first through scattered oaks and pines, then through chaparral. After about 2 miles, oaks and pines appear again.

East Mesa,
Cuyamaca
Rancho State
Park

At the junction of the Dyar Spring Trail (2.4 miles), you'll have gained almost 800 feet, already the majority of the total elevation gain during the entire trip.

Ahead lies East Mesa, more like a rolling meadow than a table-flat mesa. Keep your eyes peeled for deer; some days you may spot several at a time in this area. After passing over a low saddle you come to a junction (3.4 miles). Turn left and continue 0.6 mile to Granite Spring Primitive Camp, on the right. This is the more remote of the two trail camps in the park designated for equestrians and hikers. A hand pump at the spring dispenses potable, but somewhat unpleasant-tasting, iron-rich water.

From Granite Spring, return to the Harvey Moore Trail (which is now coincident with East Mesa Fire Rd.) and head north for another 1.0 mile to the next junction. Swing left and follow the Harvey Moore Trail north toward the deep ravine containing Harper Creek. You descend gradually at first, then quite steeply as the trail begins a zigzag course downward through a lush growth of oaks, pines, and head-high manzanita shrubs. After an elevation loss of 700 feet, you reach the bottom of the ravine, where water may or may not be flowing in Harper Creek, depending on the season and the recency of rainfall. This water should not be considered potable.

The trail turns west, darts back and forth across the creek for a short while, then climbs a little up the brushy north slope. The next 0.4 mile contours around the gorge below to avoid a particularly narrow, rocky section. Then comes the final knee-banging descent

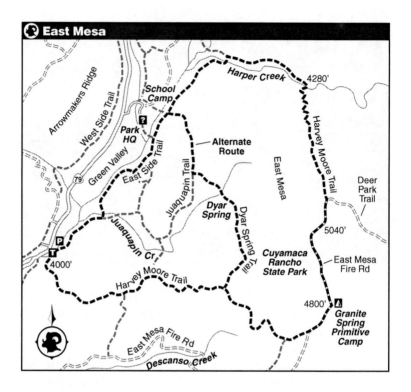

back to the level of Harper Creek. At the bottom, veer left to cross the creek, and connect with East Side Trail. As its name suggests, East Side Trail takes you back to your starting point by staying east of Highway 79—and, as it happens, along the east-side bank or flood plain of the lazily flowing Sweetwater River. The remaining 3 miles back to the Sweetwater River bridge are nearly flat and are certainly easy.

**Alternate Routes**

At 2.4 miles on the route described above, you can opt to shorten the loop considerably by turning north on Dyar Spring Trail and using it to reach East Side Trail. The resulting 6.5 mile loop has about half the elevation gain, and stays more consistently in grassland and wooded habitats, than the full Harvey Moore loop described above. You miss, however, the dramatically wild Harper Creek gorge. The clear, cold water emerging from a pipe at Dyar Spring is far more delicious than what you can get at Granite Spring.

Potable water in the East Mesa area can be found at Granite Spring **Trail Notes**
campground and at Dyar Spring (on the alternate route). There's no
water at the trailhead.

Sightings of mountain lions at Cuyamaca Rancho State Park have **Nature Notes**
become more common over the last decade. Normally secretive,
these creatures have exhibited threatening behavior toward park visitors—hikers, runners, mountain bikers, and equestrians alike. It is
recommended that you do not run alone in the park. For further
information about dealing with mountain lions, see page 11 in the
introduction to this book.

At press time, the October 2003 Cedar Fire had recently swept
across the entire Cuyamaca Rancho State Park, profoundly altering
its appearance (see p. 140).

# 41

# WEST MESA

The easy-going West Mesa route rises and falls steadily, but never too steeply, along the broad, beautifully forested flank of Cuyamaca Peak. You're on well-graded fire roads the entire way, enjoying a mix of sunshine and shade, with plenty of opportunity to sight wildlife such as deer, tree-climbing gray squirrels, and birds.

| | |
|---:|:---|
| **Distance** | 7.2 miles |
| **Time** | 1.5 to 2.5 hours |
| **Type** | Loop |
| **Elevation Gain/Loss** | 1100′/1100′ |
| **Difficulty** | Moderately strenuous |
| **Map** | Cuyamaca Rancho State Park map/brochure, available at the park's campgrounds and headquarters. USGS 7.5-min *Cuyamaca Peak* shows the topography better. |
| **Contact** | Cuyamaca Rancho State Park (760) 765-0755 |

**Trailhead Access**  Park at the day-use parking area on the east side of Highway 79 at mile 7.3. This is 7.3 miles north of Old Highway 80 near Descanso, and approximately 13 miles south of Julian.

**Route Directions**  From the parking area, head west around a gate and continue uphill on West Mesa Fire Rd. through oak and pine woods. After 0.5 mile you come to a junction. Either direction you choose at the intersection is fine since this is a loop; let's assume the counterclockwise direction. Veer right (northwest) and jog uphill through thickening stands of pine trees. Stay left at the next two trail junctions. Eventually, on the old fire road signed West Mesa Trail (and also des-

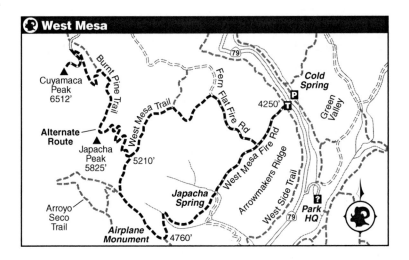

Cuyamaca Peak 6512'

Burnt Pine Trail

Alternate Route

Japacha Peak 5825'

5210'

West Mesa Trail

Fern Flat Fire Rd

4250'

Cold Spring

Green Valley

West Mesa Fire Rd

Arrowmakers Ridge

West Side Trail

Japacha Spring

Arroyo Seco Trail

Airplane Monument

4760'

Park HQ

ignated the California Riding and Hiking Trail), you begin to level off at about the 5200-foot contour.

You pass Burnt Pine Trail, a disused fire road on the right, which ascends toward the top of Cuyamaca Peak. Beyond this intersection, the West Mesa Trail starts a gentle descent across a bald spot on the mountain slope. A beautiful vista of swaying grasses, rolling hills, and distant ridges lies before you.

The descent quickens and you soon arrive at the next trail junction. Turn left and continue along the top of Airplane Ridge. After 0.9 mile, round the hairpin turn (Monument Trail junction on the right) and notice the side trail on the left leading to the Airplane Monument.

**Side Trip**

A short side trip down the Monument Trail leads to the remains of a 12-cylinder engine—part of a military aircraft that crashed at this spot in 1922.

The descent quickens again, taking you into and around a gloomy canyon and down to a junction with Japacha Fire Rd. Turn left and follow West Mesa Fire Rd. on a largely level course back to the starting point.

**Alternate Routes**

Departing from the route described above, you can ascend via Burnt Pine trail to the upper segment of the paved lookout road to Cuyamaca Peak. The wide trail switches back and forth relentlessly and is a long and tedious haul, but never becomes steep. The final 0.3 mile up the paved road to the Cuyamaca Peak summit is steep and certainly lung-busting at running pace!

**Trail Notes**  No drinking water is available either at the trailhead or en route.

**Nature Notes**  Running on West Mesa is best in April-May and October-November. Temperatures are pleasantly cool, the road surfaces are generally dry, and the forest shows off its very best leafy plumage at those two times of the year.

Sightings of mountain lions at Cuyamaca Rancho State Park have become more common over the last decade. Normally secretive, these creatures have exhibited threatening behavior toward park visitors—hikers, runners, mountain bikers, and equestrians alike. It is recommended that you do not run alone in the park. For further information about dealing with mountain lions, see page 11 in the introduction to this book.

At press time, the October 2003 Cedar Fire had recently swept across the entire Cuyamaca Rancho State Park, profoundly altering its appearance (see p. 140).

# 42

# UPPER SWEETWATER RIVER

In the south end of Cuyamaca Rancho State Park, the Sweetwater River slides placidly down a pleasant little gorge lined by alders, willows, and live oaks. Only during and after the rain or snow season does the river actually resemble its name, with a lively flow of clear and presumably sweet water. This route follows the river for some distance, and then gains higher ground in chaparral and oak country agreeably scented with blossoms in the springtime.

|  |  |
|---|---|
| **Distance** | 7.2 miles |
| **Time** | 1.5 to 2.5 hours |
| **Type** | Loop |
| **Elevation Gain/Loss** | 700´/700´ |
| **Difficulty** | Moderate |
| **Map** | Cuyamaca Rancho State Park map/brochure, available at the park's campgrounds and headquarters. USGS 7.5-min *Cuyamaca Peak* shows the topography better. |
| **Contact** | Cuyamaca Rancho State Park (760) 765-0755 |

**Trailhead Access**

To reach the starting point from Interstate 8 near Descanso, drive north 2.7 miles on Highway 79 and turn left (north) toward Cuyamaca Rancho State Park, staying on 79. After another 0.2 mile, turn left on Viejas Blvd. Continue 1.1 miles to a trailhead parking lot next to a ranger residence on the right.

**Route Directions**

Starting from the parking lot, go past a vehicle gate. The Merigan Fire Rd., flat at first and easy for running, takes you across a sunny meadow, then up onto a brushy slope. In springtime, the air rising along the slopes bears both the tangy fragrance of new growth in the

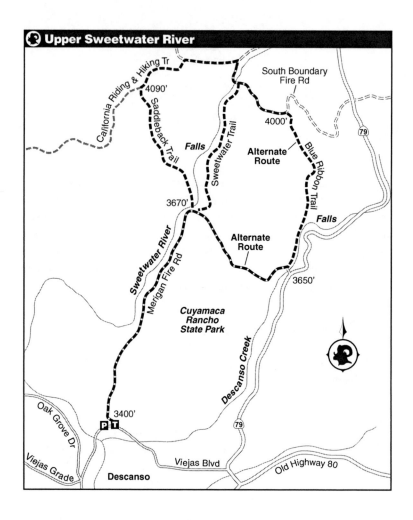

California Riding & Hiking Tr

4090'

Saddleback Trail

Falls

Sweetwater Trail

South Boundary
Fire Rd

4000'

Alternate
Route

Blue Ribbon Trail

79

Falls

3670'

Sweetwater River

Merigan Fire Rd

Alternate
Route

3650'

Cuyamaca
Rancho
State Park

Descanso Creek

Oak Grove Dr

3400'

P T

79

Viejas Grade

Viejas Blvd

Old Highway 80

Descanso

chaparral and the humid scent of the stream-hugging willows just ahead. Blue ceanothus paints the brushy hillsides in April through early May.

Stay on the fire road, keeping to the right (east side) of the Sweetwater River. You cross two side trails, which branch left and dip to cross the river and its accompanying strip of riparian vegetation. After some further climbing, you enter a magnificent grove of live oak trees and sidle up close to the high bank of the creek. Down below, through a screen of willows and alders, the ice-cold Sweetwater sparkles as it tumbles over the gravelly canyon floor.

At 1.9 miles, you reach a junction of trails in flat area dotted with oaks and a few pines. Crossing the river there, you pick up the Saddleback Trail, which takes you uphill and northwest to the California Riding and Hiking Trail (3.1 miles). During March this slope is alive with the drone of bees frantically gathering nectar from the blooming manzanitas.

Make a right turn onto the California Riding and Hiking Trail, a right on South Boundary Fire Rd., another right to stay on South Boundary Fire Rd., and a fourth right on the Sweetwater Trail (4.2 miles). This section is relatively devoid of tall vegetation, so you'll have spacious views of the higher Cuyamaca Mountains, but at the expense of running in hot midday sunshine. Sweetwater Trail will take you down along the semi-shaded east slope of the Sweetwater gorge, at times almost 100 feet above the water. At 5.3 miles you'll arrive back at Merigan Fire Rd.; follow it back to the trailhead.

**Alternate Routes**

As an alternate to the loop described above, you can try this slightly longer loop with a little less elevation gain: At 1.9 miles, instead of crossing the river, continue on Merigan Fire Rd. as it turns east toward Highway 79. Just short of the vehicle gate near the highway, turn north and follow the Blue Ribbon Trail, going up a drainage toward South Boundary Fire Rd. Take the latter down to the bank of the Sweetwater River and turn left on the trail going down the Sweetwater gorge.

**Trail Notes**

There's no potable water available at the trailhead or along the route.

**Nature Notes**

Sightings of mountain lions at Cuyamaca Rancho State Park have become more common over the last decade. Normally secretive, these creatures have exhibited threatening behavior toward park visitors—hikers, runners, mountain bikers, and equestrians alike. It is recommended that you do not run alone in the park. For further information about dealing with mountain lions, see page 11 in the introduction to this book.

At press time, the October 2003 Cedar Fire had recently swept across the entire Cuyamaca Rancho State Park, profoundly altering its appearance (see p. 140).

# 43

## NOBLE CANYON

From an easily reached trailhead near Pine Valley, the popular Noble Canyon Trail ascends toward the crest of the Laguna Mountains. This looping route, which stays mostly in the warmer chaparral belt, is ideal for late fall through spring. Avoid the heat of summer days—unless of course you are interested in heat acclimation!

| | |
|---|---|
| **Distance** | 12.5 miles |
| **Time** | 3 to 5 hours |
| **Type** | Loop |
| **Elevation Gain/Loss** | 2300′/2300′ |
| **Difficulty** | Strenuous |
| **Map** | USGS 7.5-min *Descanso, Mount Laguna, Monument Peak, Cuyamaca Peak* |
| **Contact** | Cleveland National Forest, Descanso Ranger District (619) 445-6235 |

**Trailhead Access**  Exit Interstate 8 at Highway 79 about 35 miles east of San Diego. Go north on Highway 79 and continue straight as the 79 route turns north after 2.7 miles. Drive another 4 miles through the community of Guatay and down a long grade. Turn left at the bottom of the grade on Pine Creek Rd. (next to a bridge over Pine Creek Rd.). Continue 1.6 miles north to the Noble Canyon trailhead on the right.

**Route Directions**  Noble Canyon Trail wastes no time on the ascent as it heads generally east on a chaparral-covered slope. The entire trail is popular with mountain bikers, but this initial section is so eroded down to uneven bedrock that some bikers like to walk their bikes through here. Even going uphill, runners must use caution on this ankle-busting terrain.

After 1 mile, the trail rolls over a summit and begins a very pleasant, gradual descent into Noble Canyon on smooth, decomposed granite soil. At times, it seems, you can almost fly. At 2.5 miles, you

Laguna Meadow
in springtime

cross the rocky canyon bottom and stream, and pick up the continuation of the Noble Canyon Trail on the far (north) bank a short way up the slope. Don't be confused by informal "use" trails that go down Noble Canyon on both sides of the creek, heading back to Pine Creek Rd. Our route continues upstream (east) through the canyon, but generally 50 or 100 feet above the level of the creek. In the next mile, the trail is rocky at times, and the low-growing chaparral and open sun exposure contributes to a desert-like feel. Yucca, prickly-pear cactus, and even hedgehog cactus—normally found in the desert many miles east—grow on the slopes above and below the trail.

You pass an old mine tunnel at 3.3 miles, and by 3.9 miles dip to cross the creek. Just upslope from this spot, on the right, are old cabin foundations—a good spot to rest or snack, but be mindful of the poison oak in this area. To the left of the creek crossing a meadow gently rises. On the upper edge of this meadow you can find the remains of a disused dirt road leading uphill to Pine Creek Rd.—a possible way to turn your run into a shorter loop if you feel you need to bail out.

---

Though evidence is increasingly scant, just up the side-branching trail to Pine Creek Rd. are the remains of a flume and various mining relics dating from a flurry of gold-mining activity in the region during the late 1800s.

*Mini Gold Rush*

---

Our way, however, continues uphill, steeply at times, through a narrow section of Noble Canyon agreeably shaded by live oaks and

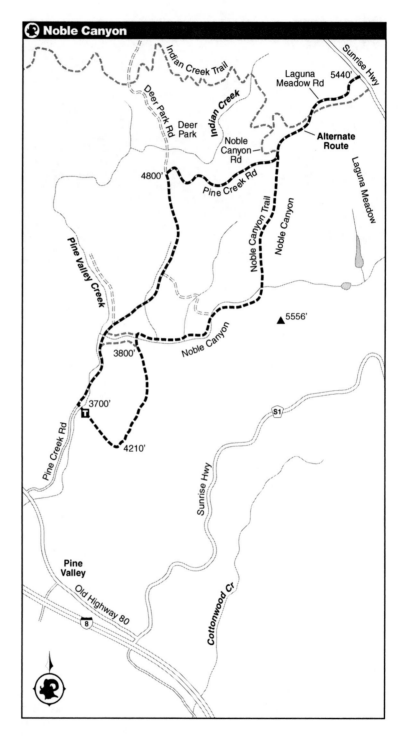

Indian Creek Trail

Sunrise Hwy

Deer Park Rd

Indian Creek

Laguna Meadow Rd

5440'

Deer Park

Noble Canyon Rd

**Alternate Route**

Pine Creek Rd

4800'

Laguna Meadow

Noble Canyon Trail

Noble Canyon

Pine Valley Creek

▲5556'

Noble Canyon

3800'

3700'

S1

4210'

Pine Creek Rd

Sunrise Hwy

Pine Valley

Old Highway 80

8

Cottonwood Cr

most notably California bay trees—which exude an ineffably sweet-pungent scent. The happily bubbling creek lies on the left now, mostly hidden by tall willows and sycamores, and low-growing wild strawberry vines, wild rose bushes, and a poison-oak look-alike called Indian basket bush. Be aware that some of that trailside vegetation is in fact poison oak!

At 4.8 miles you cross an often-wet tributary of Noble Canyon that drains the Laguna Meadow area to the east. It's worth a pause to catch your breath here and appreciate the water sliding around grayish boulders and gathering in fern-fringed pools that reflect the leafy canopy above. Onward the climb continues, alternately in sun-struck chaparral or under the twisting limbs of live oaks and black oaks. Jeffrey pines become more common as you gain elevation.

At 6.5 miles you reach Pine Creek Rd. To follow our designated loop route, turn left here and use Pine Creek Rd. to get back to the starting point. After you reach a high point of just over a mile in elevation (5330 feet) on Pine Creek Rd., your return to the trailhead is almost entirely downhill. Despite the lack of spectacular scenery on the last 6-mile segment of graded-dirt, graveled, and asphalt roadway, you will get back to your car quickly this way as long as you continue at running pace.

**Alternate Routes**

With a drop-off and pick-up arrangement, you could run the entire Noble Canyon Trail in either the uphill or the downhill direction, just over 9 miles one-way if you stick to the trail all the way. Using the upper part of Laguna Meadow Rd. instead shortens the distance to about 8 miles.

Furthermore, it is possible to short-cut the lowermost 2.5 miles of Noble Canyon Trail by heading east, using the informal "use" trails mentioned above, to get from Pine Creek Rd. to the main Noble Canyon Trail.

**Trail Notes**

Drinking water is available at the trailhead, but not along any part of the route. The Noble Canyon Trail is often rocky and rutted, so wear appropriate footwear and watch your step.

**Nature Notes**

The Noble Canyon Trail is a regionally famous, downhill "kamikaze" mountain-biking route. If you don't particularly enjoy sudden encounters with two-wheeled machines, then try running the trail on a weekday when the route is practically deserted.

# 44

## OLD COUNTY ROAD

Old County and Agua Dulce Creek roads are barely noted on maps or in tourist literature about the Laguna Mountains, but they're perfect for runners wanting to get some mountain training without excessively steep grades. Stringing the two roads together in a loop involves a passage through Laguna Meadow, which is often too soggy to cross between December and March, but usually firm and dry enough the rest of the year.

|  |  |
|---:|:---|
| **Distance** | 5.3 miles |
| **Time** | 1 to 2 hours |
| **Type** | Loop |
| **Elevation Gain/Loss** | 600'/600' |
| **Difficulty** | Moderate |
| **Map** | USGS 7.5-min *Monument Peak* |
| **Contact** | Cleveland National Forest, Descanso Ranger District (619) 445-6235 |

**Trailhead Access** Park along the wide shoulder of Sunrise Highway at or near the Meadows Information Station (kiosk), mile 19.1, about 5 miles uphill from Interstate 8 at Pine Valley. This parking area serves as the trailhead for the Sunset Trail.

**Route Directions** From the information station, proceed 0.2 mile uphill along the shoulder of Sunrise Highway—or just off the road in the pine forest—to the second gated road intersecting on the left (north). That second gated road, the "Old County Road," is an abandoned segment of the original road that climbed into the Lagunas. Follow it gradually uphill, sometimes on dirt and sometimes on crumbling macadam, enjoying the solitude of the oak and pine forest. Chances are you'll encounter no one else.

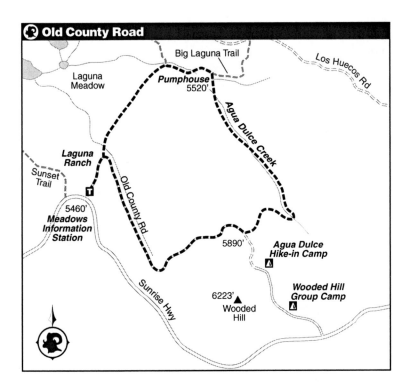

Big Laguna Trail

Los Huecos Rd

Laguna
Meadow

**Pumphouse
5520'**

Agua Dulce Creek

**Laguna
Ranch**

Sunset
Trail

Old County Rd

5460'
**Meadows
Information
Station**

5890'

**Agua Dulce
Hike-in Camp**

Sunrise Hwy

6223'
Wooded
Hill

**Wooded Hill
Group Camp**

After 2.1 miles, the Old County Road passes over a summit and begins a slight descent. Look for a narrow dirt road—more like a wide trail—going through a gap in the barbed-wire fence on the left. (If you reach the entrance to Agua Dulce Hike-in Camp, you've gone too far). Follow that narrow dirt road as it abruptly veers right and begins to descend into the straight and narrow ravine of Agua Dulce Creek. Not much water flows here, but enough moisture collects in this north-flowing drainage to support incense-cedars, as well as the usual black oaks and Jeffrey pines found throughout the Laguna range.

Keep following the ravine bottom on the same, narrow dirt road, heading gradually downhill. At 3.6 miles, you come upon a disused pumphouse, part of a water system that served the now-defunct Mount Laguna air force radar station on Stephenson Peak. The old road ends here. Simply push ahead through the grassy bottomland beyond (Boiling Spring Ravine), and hook up with the well-worn Big Laguna Trail on the ravine's far side. Turn left, and follow that trail westward toward the broad south arm of Laguna Meadow, a short distance away.

After passing through a narrow gate at the edge of the meadow, you'll soon need to leave the Big Laguna Trail. Veer left in order to bee-line south or southwest across the meadow toward your starting point. The cluster of buildings at Laguna Ranch is a good visual guide for the direction you should travel. Head left of the ranch buildings to return to the lower part of Old County Rd., or head right to return more directly to the start of the Sunset Trail and your parked car. The right-side route may be more soggy if the ground is wet. Either way, watch your footing when covering the uneven ground—or you can simply walk the last mile as a cool-down. During the warmer months, cattle graze in the meadow; they don't pay much attention to recreational visitors passing through.

**Alternate Routes**  You can add about 5 miles, and not much elevation gain or loss, to your loop by sticking with the Big Laguna Trail once you reach Laguna Meadow, following that trail north about 2 miles to Sunset Trail, and using Sunset Trail to return to the starting point.

**Trail Notes**  No water is available, either at the trailhead or along the route.

Early morning in Laguna Meadow

# 45

# BIG LAGUNA LOOP

The Big Laguna loop route wiggles through the transition zone
between the forested upper Laguna Mountains and the raw desert
below, offering ever-changing perspectives of the land, the sky, and
distant horizons. You never dip below 5400 feet of elevation nor rise
to more than 5900 feet, so the course is decent for altitude training.
The well-traveled trails are consistently single-track width, which
means that you're always in close sensory contact with the surround-
ing fragrant forest and chaparral vegetation. You're likely to
encounter mountain bikers on the Big Laguna Trail portion of the
run, but bikes are not allowed on the Pacific Crest Trail segment.

|  |  |
|---|---|
| **Distance** | 10.0 miles |
| **Time** | 2 to 3 hours |
| **Type** | Loop |
| **Elevation Gain/Loss** | 900´/900´ |
| **Difficulty** | Moderately strenuous |
| **Map** | USGS 7.5-min *Monument Peak* |
| **Contact** | Cleveland National Forest, Descanso Ranger District (619) 445-6235 |

**Trailhead Access**

The Penny Pines roadside parking area, at mile 27.3 on Sunrise
Highway, is a good place to begin. To reach it, drive about 13 miles
north from Interstate 8 or about 10 miles south from the Highway
79/Sunrise Highway intersection, near Cuyamaca Reservoir.

**Route Directions**

From the parking area, go west on the Noble Canyon Trail through
oak and pine forest. After only 0.1 mile, there's a split: you go left on
the Big Laguna Trail (BLT). After a short mile, the BLT breaks out of
the woods and turns south to skirt the margin of Laguna Meadow.
Keep going straight as Sunset Trail branches right. By 2.5 miles into
the so-far easy run, you'll be opposite Big Laguna Lake. This long,

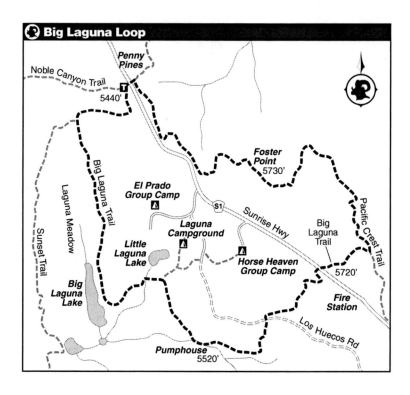

**Big Laguna Loop**

Penny Pines

Noble Canyon Trail

5440'

Foster Point 5730'

Big Laguna Trail

El Prado Group Camp

Laguna Meadow

S1

Sunrise Hwy

Big Laguna Trail

Laguna Campground

Pacific Crest Trail

Sunset Trail

Little Laguna Lake

Horse Heaven Group Camp

5720'

Big Laguna Lake

Fire Station

Los Huecos Rd

Pumphouse 5520'

skinny pond is one of a handful of shallow depressions in Laguna Meadow that hold water during part or all of the year, depending solely on recent rainfall or snow.

Next, the trail turns east toward an arm of Laguna Meadow that contains Little Laguna Lake. When you reach a wire fence at 2.8 miles, don't go through the gap in the fence. Instead, turn abruptly right and follow the fenceline over to the wooded area on the meadow's east side. A spur trail branches left toward Laguna Campground, where water is available if you need it.

The main trail continues south along the meadow edge and then east to follow a shallow ravine. Off to the right you'll spot a disused pumphouse at the mouth of the Agua Dulce Creek ravine (see the previous run description for more details about the "Old County" route that goes that way).

After a turn to the north and a short bit of steep climbing, you cross the graded Los Huecos Rd. (4.5 miles) and hook up with an old roadbed going east and later north. You ascend easily through chaparral—mostly ceanothus, which puts on a great floral show in

Laguna
Mountains from
the PCT

the late spring. Look for the shiny-leafed chokecherry bushes, which may bear prodigious quantities of ripe red fruit in the fall.

When the roadbed makes a hairpin turn to the right (at 5.0 miles), stay left on the footpath that continues through a gap in a wire fence. You swoop down through more pine and oak woods, cross Sunrise Highway, and continue east, uphill, to join the Pacific Crest Trail (PCT) at 6.0 miles.

Turn left on the PCT and return to your starting point by way of a rambling but scenic stretch of the PCT. You'll traverse through mixed pine/oak forest and through the narrow belt of chaparral that separates the Laguna forest from the top of the desert-facing escarpment. Along the way, on the right side of the trail, you can take advantage of several overlooks offering sweeping views of the desert.

**Trail Notes**    You'll be on single-track trails almost the entire way, smooth except for certain rock-strewn sections of the PCT. Drinking water is available only at Laguna Campground, slightly off the route.

The northern part of this route was burned in the 2003 Cedar Fire (see p. 140). Parts of the desert-facing (east-facing) slopes of the Laguna Mountains were burned earlier, in the 2002 Pines Fire.

# 46

# INDIAN CREEK LOOP

Like the previous run, this one samples a variety of appealing environments amid some of the highest elevations in San Diego County. You'll tramp through shady oak and pine woods, spice-scented chaparral, and sage-dotted meadows. Plus, from various vantage points along the Pacific Crest Trail, you'll get some spacious views of the Anza-Borrego Desert to the north.

| | |
|---|---|
| **Distance** | 8.0 miles |
| **Time** | 2 to 3 hours |
| **Type** | Loop |
| **Elevation Gain/Loss** | 1000´/1000´ |
| **Difficulty** | Moderately strenuous |
| **Map** | USGS 7.5-min *Monument Peak* |
| **Contact** | Cleveland National Forest, Descanso Ranger District (619) 445-6235 |

**Trailhead Access**

The Penny Pines roadside parking area, at mile 27.3 on Sunrise Highway, is a good place to begin. To reach it, drive about 13 miles north from Interstate 8 or about 10 miles south from the Highway 79/Sunrise Highway intersection near Cuyamaca Reservoir.

**Route Directions**

Start by following the Noble Canyon Trail west through Jeffrey-pine forest. You gain the north slope of a hill and then drop to cross unpaved roads three times. After one more ascent circling around the north end of a ridge, you'll come to a junction with the Indian Creek Trail, 2.4 miles from the start. Turn right at this junction and descend about 0.8 mile through black oaks and chaparral to the grassy banks along trickling (or possibly dry) Indian Creek.

On the far bank, Indian Creek Trail swings west to crookedly ascend the flank of Pine Mountain. Up the bank a short way, you leave that trail and veer right (north) on the unsigned remnants of an

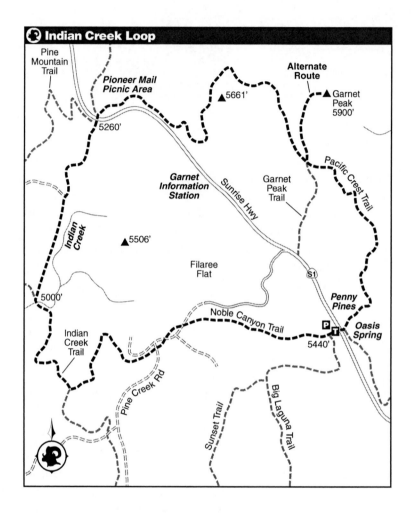

**Indian Creek Loop**

Pine Mountain Trail

Pioneer Mail Picnic Area

Alternate Route

▲5661'

▲ Garnet Peak 5900'

5260'

Pacific Crest Trail

Garnet Information Station

Sunrise Hwy

Garnet Peak Trail

Indian Creek

▲5506'

Filaree Flat

S1

5000'

Penny Pines

Noble Canyon Trail

Indian Creek Trail

Oasis Spring

5440'

Pine Creek Rd

Sunset Trail

Big Laguna Trail

old dirt road that stays high above and to the left of Indian Creek. Keep going on what becomes a better dirt road (though very steep and eroded in one spot) until you reach Pioneer Mail Picnic Area, 4.6 miles, on the far side of Sunrise Highway. Pick up the Pacific Crest Trail (PCT), which passes downslope of the picnic tables, and head east, parallel to Sunrise Highway. The Pines Fire roared through here in 2002, burning just about everything below the picnic ground to a crisp, but in the next several years, new growth should greatly improve the landscape appearance.

After jogging a few minutes alongside the highway, the PCT starts curling left, rising on oak- and pine-shaded hillsides often dotted with colorful spring or early-summer wildflowers. Then you contour around a blackened slope with wide-open views of the desert-mountain interface to the north. Post-fire spring wildflowers could make these burned spaces very colorful for the next two or three years. At 6.8 miles the PCT intersects a trail slanting upward toward the summit of Garnet Peak. You, however, maintain a near-level course on the PCT that takes you along the rim of the desert-facing escarpment. Just east of the trail in several spots, you can walk out to the very brink of the escarpment and gaze downward upon the desert floor. A final descent on the PCT, through oaks and pines, takes you back to the Penny Pines plantation and your car.

**Alternate Routes**

As an addition to the route above—rather than as an alternative—follow the Garnet Peak trail out-and-back to the rocky summit of Garnet Peak. That summit offers the single best perspective in the Lagunas for viewing the desert landscape. The run or hike to and from Garnet Peak adds 1.2 miles and 400 feet of elevation gain to your 8-mile loop.

**Trail Notes**

No water is available at the trailhead or along the route.

The October 2003 Cedar Fire (see p. 140) burned across much of the landscape traversed by the Indian Creek Loop, finally coming to a halt at the border of the 2002 Pines Fire area.

Canyon in the Carrizo Badlands

# THE DESERT

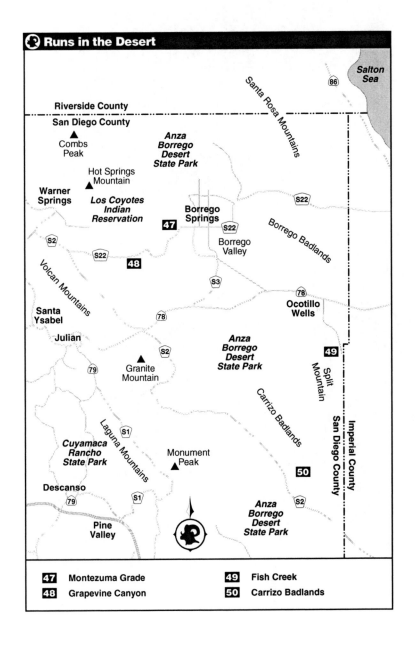

**Runs in the Desert**

Salton Sea

86

Santa Rosa Mountains

Riverside County

San Diego County

▲ Combs Peak

*Anza Borrego Desert State Park*

Hot Springs ▲ Mountain

**Warner Springs**

*Los Coyotes Indian Reservation*

**Borrego Springs**

S22

47

S22

Borrego Valley

Borrego Badlands

S2

S22

48

S3

Volcan Mountains

**Santa Ysabel**

78

78

**Ocotillo Wells**

**Julian**

79

S2

*Anza Borrego Desert State Park*

49

Split Mountain

▲ Granite Mountain

Carrizo Badlands

San Diego County

Imperial County

Laguna Mountains

S1

*Cuyamaca Rancho State Park*

Monument ▲ Peak

**Descanso**

79

S1

50

**Pine Valley**

*Anza Borrego Desert State Park*

S2

| | |
|---|---|
| **47** Montezuma Grade | **49** Fish Creek |
| **48** Grapevine Canyon | **50** Carrizo Badlands |

# 47

# MONTEZUMA GRADE

Visitors approaching Borrego Springs and the Anza-Borrego Desert from the west on Montezuma Highway (Highway S-22) are always impressed by the final, spectacular, winding, and sharply descending passage down the Montezuma Grade. The California Riding and Hiking Trail traverses a fair distance north of that highway, and its similar route is just as remarkable. For runners, it may seem that the direction to go on the trail would be one-way downhill—but that logic is belied by the fact that this often-rocky and sometimes-steep trail in cactus country is potentially dangerous for downhill running. So give your knees a break and your lungs a good strong workout by traveling the trail in the (ugh!) uphill direction.

| | |
|---:|:---|
| **Distance** | 8.0 miles |
| **Time** | 3 to 5 hours |
| **Type** | Point to point |
| **Elevation Gain/Loss** | 3700′ / 500′ |
| **Difficulty** | Strenuous |
| **Map** | USGS 7.5-min *Tubb Canyon* |
| **Contact** | Anza-Borrego Desert State Park |
| | (760) 767-5311 or (760) 767-4205 |

**Trailhead Access**

The top of the trail is at mile 6.8, across Montezuma Highway (Highway S-22) from the junction of the signed Jasper Trail. The bottom terminus, and presumably your starting point, is the large trailhead parking area on the west side of Montezuma Highway, 0.7 mile south of Palm Canyon Dr. in Borrego Springs.

**Route Directions**

Starting off from the bottom trailhead, within a few minutes you commence a breathless, zigzag ascent up a dry slope, gaining 500 feet in elevation. That gets you to a saddle on an east-west trending ridge. You turn right and follow that ridge west.

Opposite page:
Anza-Borrego Desert

| _Historical_ | Most of this route is virtually coincident with a pathway originally used as a |
|:---|:---|
| _Highway_ | mountain-desert travel corridor for prehistoric Native Americans, and later |
| | used by cowboys driving cattle herds between the mountain meadows |
| | and the desert floor. |

You continue up or along that ridge for several miles, through a habitat shift from low-desert to high-desert. Early on, note the spindly ocotillos, spine-tipped agaves, various low-growing but vicious cacti such as chollas, pungent-scented creosote bushes, and yellow-flowering brittlebushes. Higher up you'll be in the chaparral vegetation belt, and higher still you'll encounter a bit of the juniper and pinyon-pine belt. At every elevation level, the view is outstanding—ever-changing and always fascinating. On clear days, mountain ranges 50 to 100 miles away can be seen in the north and east.

At 4.5 miles, the trail rolls over the bald spot on the ridge, dubbed "the Lookout" or "View Point," that is easily accessible from Culp Valley Campground just south. Pressing on, you swoop briefly downhill, then uphill for a while, then sharply downhill once more. At the bottom of that last dip (the uppermost reaches of South Fork Hellhole Canyon) you cross the Pena Spring trail.

Pena Spring, 0.3 mile to the right, offers a possible potable source of water; however, the Pines Fire of 2002 destroyed the spring box and piping here, and water may be hard to collect from the oozing acre or so that you'll find here.

From now on you're in a partially burned zone. You proceed uphill for about 2 more miles, winding amid bouldered hillsides and peaklets, to a low saddle. Beyond that, the trail levels out and runs straight to the upper trailhead on Montezuma Highway.

**Alternate** If you don't mind running downhill on Montezuma Highway, you
**Routes** can use a 10-mile segment of this two-lane road to return to the bottom trailhead. Or, do the downhill road-run first, and loop back uphill on the trail. Don't consider doing this unless traffic is light, typically on a weekday, or else do it very early in the morning. Note that in California pedestrians (runners included) are supposed to travel on the left side of the highway, facing oncoming traffic. You may also use Montezuma Highway to loop back to Pena Spring or Culp Valley campground.

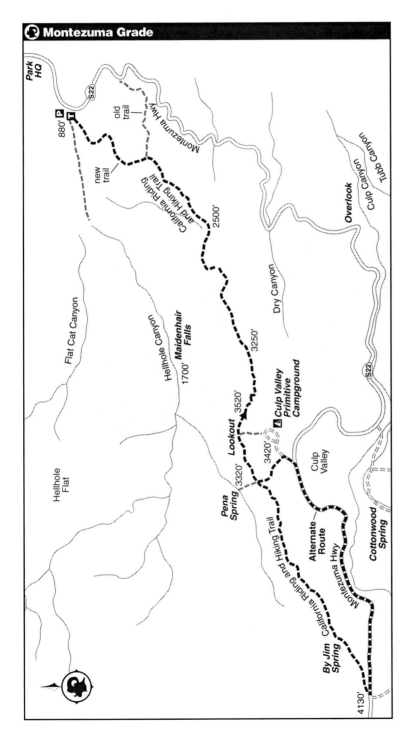

# Montezuma Grade

Park HQ

S22

880'

old trail

new trail

Montezuma Hwy

California Riding and Hiking Trail

2500'

Flat Cat Canyon

Hellhole Canyon

Maidenhair Falls

1700'

Hellhole Flat

3250'

Dry Canyon

Overlook

Culp Canyon

Tubb Canyon

S22

Lookout

3520'

Culp Valley Primitive Campground

3420'

Culp Valley

Pena Spring

3320'

California Riding and Hiking Trail

Alternate Route

Montezuma Hwy

Cottonwood Spring

By Jim Spring

4130'

The Desert **179**

**Trail Notes**    No water is available at either the start or end. Even though there's some surface water at Pena Spring, just off-route, carry all the water you think you will need. Parts of the trail are steep and exceedingly rocky.

**Nature Notes**    Avoiding the desert heat is the surely the hottest tip in these parts. The middle elevations encountered on this run may be comfortable for running only during November through March. You'll need to carry plenty of water—even if temperature rises no higher than 70°F.

Sunrise on the Calif. Riding and Hiking Trail

# 48

# GRAPEVINE CANYON

The Jasper Trail to Grapevine Canyon jeep-route takes hikers, runners, and travelers on wheels down a series of inclines from Anza-Borrego's cool, western margins to its warm, dry interior. Despite the overall descent of some 2400 feet of elevation, this isn't exactly a Sunday picnic for anyone, especially since the route offers almost no shade. Convince someone to drop you off at the start and pick you up later at the finish.

| | |
|---|---|
| **Distance** | 11.0 miles |
| **Time** | 2.5 to 4 hours |
| **Type** | Point to point |
| **Elevation Gain/Loss** | 500′/2900′ |
| **Difficulty** | Moderately strenuous |
| **Map** | USGS 7.5-min *Tubb Canyon, Ranchita* |
| **Contact** | Anza-Borrego Desert State Park |
| | (760) 767-5311 or (760) 767-4205 |

**Trailhead Access**

The starting point is the north terminus of the Jasper Trail (a Jeep road), mile 6.8 on the Montezuma Highway (Highway S-22) east of Ranchita. The route ends on Highway 78 at mile 74.1, about 3 miles west of Tamarisk Grove Campground.

**Route Directions**

In the first couple of miles the narrow, unpaved road (Jasper Trail) traverses rolling, brushy terrain, generally heading south. After passing over a rocky ridge at 2.4 miles, the road drops very sharply down a dry canyon for about 0.7 mile; then it turns north up a slope and briefly follows a ridge to avoid a narrow, rocky section of the canyon. On foot it's easier to walk (not run) down the bottom of that canyon instead of following the road, and then rejoin the road. You'll save 0.4 mile, not to mention needless elevation gain and loss.

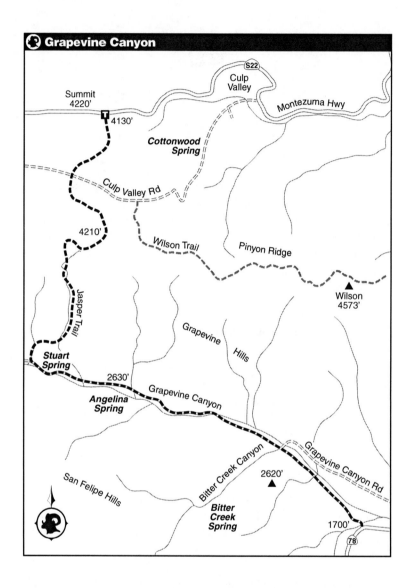

**Grapevine Canyon**

Summit
4220'

4130'

Culp
Valley

S22

Montezuma Hwy

Cottonwood
Spring

Culp Valley Rd

4210'

Wilson Trail

Pinyon Ridge

Wilson
4573'

Jasper Trail

Grapevine

Hills

Stuart
Spring

2630'

Grapevine Canyon

Angelina
Spring

Grapevine Canyon Rd

San Felipe Hills

Bitter Creek Canyon

2620'

Bitter
Creek
Spring

1700'

78

In the next mile, the canyon is flanked by picturesque, near-vertical
rock walls. After some further twists and turns and ups and downs,
you arrive at the broad floor of Grapevine Canyon.

Follow the dirt road (or, at times, a paralleling equestrian and hiking trail) down the broad floor of Grapevine Canyon. You pass
Angelina Spring, recognizable by a thicket of willows. Where the
wide Bitter Creek Canyon comes in from the south, the road forks
and Grapevine Canyon Rd. veers left toward Yaqui Well and

Tamarisk Grove Campground. You stay to the right, as this road leads more directly to Highway 78, 2 miles away, which is where, hopefully, your driver or car awaits you.

---

*In the Canyon*

Before the completion of Highway 78, Grapevine Canyon was a principal east-west route of travel. Several springs in the canyon served the needs of early automobile travelers—but today you can't depend on them for potable water. Centuries ago, Grapevine Canyon was a favorite camping area of Native Americans. Here and there you might find bedrock mortars, used for the grinding of seeds and grain.

---

**Trail Notes**

Don't count on finding water anywhere along the route. You'll encounter some ORV or jeep traffic, especially in Grapevine Canyon.

**Nature Notes**

Outside of the prime daytime desert visitation season (November through March), this one-way route should only be attempted during early morning or perhaps on the evening of a full moon. Carry plenty of water.

# 49

# FISH CREEK

Anza-Borrego's Fish Creek Wash is the main gateway to a fascinating labyrinth of rugged canyons, twisted arroyos, and mud hills covering the desiccated area known as the Carrizo Badlands. At one time, desert pupfish eked out a marginal existence in shallow ponds here, but today, the broad, sandy floor of Fish Creek supports only scattered drought-tolerant vegetation and a sporadic stream of travelers by foot and SUV.

| | |
|---:|:---|
| **Distance** | Up to 13 miles one way |
| **Type** | Out and back |
| **Elevation Gain/Loss** | 1000 feet steady gain in 13 miles one-way |
| **Difficulty** | Moderate to strenuous (if 26-mile "marathon" round-trip distance is attempted) |
| **Map** | Anza-Borrego Desert State Park visitors map, available at the park's visitor center in Borrego Springs |
| **Contact** | Anza-Borrego Desert State Park (760) 767-5311 or (760) 767-4205 |

**Trailhead Access** From Highway 78 at Ocotillo Wells, go 8 miles south on the paved Split Mountain Rd. to the dirt-road turnoff for Fish Creek Campground. This is the presumed starting point—though drivers in passenger cars usually can drive in more than a mile, and sturdier vehicles may be able to negotiate the entire 13-mile-long route.

**Route Directions** About 2 miles from the paved Split Mountain Rd., you reach the looming portals of Split Mountain. The waters of Fish Creek Wash (in rare flood stage, at least) have worn their way through a fault zone, creating sheer walls on both sides. The next 2 miles are unarguably

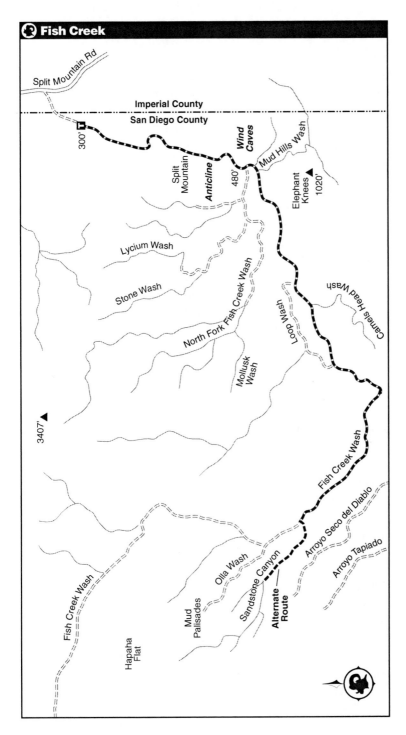

Split Mountain Rd

Split Mountain Rd

**Imperial County**

**San Diego County**

300'

Split Mountain

*Anticline*

480'

*Wind Caves*

Mud Hills Wash

Elephant Knees
1020'

Camals Head Wash

Lycium Wash

Stone Wash

North Fork Fish Creek Wash

Loop Wash

Mollusk Wash

3407'

Fish Creek Wash

Fish Creek Wash

Olla Wash

Sandstone Canyon

Arroyo Seco del Diablo

Arroyo Tapiado

**Alternate Route**

Mud Palisades

Hapaha Flat

spectacular, with the bare bones of the earth exposed in all of its geologic complexity.

---

*Split Mountain*  On the right, just before the walls of Split Mountain begin to part away,
*Anticline*  don't miss a spectacular anticline (an inverted U) of sandstone layers
embedded in the canyon wall. An interpretive panel on a rise opposite this
feature presents the latest geological thinking about how it may have
formed. Casual runners may want to turn around at this point.

---

You continue into a landscape dominated by "mud hills" strewn with sparkling chips of gypsum crystal. Stick with the main Fish Creek route, staying in the main wash all the while. Keep on truckin' gradually upward—if you have the mettle—all the way to the confluence of Sandstone Canyon, 13.4 miles from the pavement by way of the wheel tracks. There are some opportunities for short-cuts across the wash that can reduce that distance to about 13 miles.) The Fish Creek route continues north from there, but goes through less interesting and more severely inclined terrain ahead. The mouth of Sandstone Canyon is therefore a good place to turn around and take advantage of a modest boost from gravity on the return leg.

**Alternate**  Any good map of Anza-Borrego desert features shows the many
**Routes**  tributaries of Fish Creek, some threaded with roads, others unroaded but still runnable. The partially roaded Sandstone Canyon is the best of them all. Roadside camping is allowed throughout the area, so a weekend "running vacation" may be required to more fully explore the route options.

**Trail Notes**  There's no water within miles of the trailhead, so fill up at home, or at Ocotillo Wells as you approach the trailhead.

**Nature Notes**  The Fish Creek area lies in one of the hottest and also the driest low-elevation basins of the world, so the season for running here is quite short. December through February is best. Needless to say, there's normally not a drop of water to drink anywhere out here.

Rare, heavy rain can wet the canyon floor to such an extent that forward momentum is a messy and glacially slow process. When dry, however, Fish Creek Wash has stretches of soft sand to contend with.

Conditions are ideal when there's just a little moisture on the ground to firm up the otherwise soft sand.

Slot canyon, Arroyo Seco del Diablo (Run 50)

# 50

## CARRIZO BADLANDS

This looping route through the Carrizo Badlands of southern Anza-Borrego Desert State Park introduces you to the most bizarre terrain in San Diego County and features spectacular examples of erosion in soft claystones, mudstones, and sandstones. As you run along, mostly on smooth roads of packed sand, you'll marvel at the endless variations of clay hills, mud caves, small arches and windows, receding cliffs, sinuous washes, and deep-cut ravines. You'll follow Arroyo Tapiado uphill and then descend through Arroyo Seco del Diablo.

|  |  |
|---:|:---|
| **Distance** | 16.5 miles |
| **Time** | 4 to 5.5 hours |
| **Type** | Loop |
| **Elevation Gain/Loss** | 600′/600′ |
| **Difficulty** | Moderately strenuous |
| **Map** | USGS 7.5-min *Arroyo Tapiado* |
| **Contact** | Anza-Borrego Desert State Park (760) 767-5311 or (760) 767-4205 |

**Trailhead Access** Find the signed Palm Spring turnoff near mile marker 43.0 on County Highway S-2. Drive off the pavement and east down the broad Vallecito Wash, staying in the main (unsigned) wash when the spur road to Palm Spring forks left. At 4.5 miles from S-2, a small sign on the left marks Arroyo Tapiado, a broad, shallow, and uninteresting drainage at this point. This is as good a spot as any to begin your run.

**Route Directions** On foot, proceed north along Arroyo Tapiado (meaning "mudwall wash"). After 2.0 miles you reach the beginning of a deep, twisting gorge.

Vallecito Mountains, rising north of the Carrizo Badlands

*Pseudokarst*

After the first 2 miles up the Arroyo Tapiado wash, you pass through 2 miles of what geologists call pseudokarst topography. Similar to the limestone karst topography found in many parts of the world, pseudokarst contains caves, subterranean drainage systems, sinkholes, and blind valleys that end in swallow holes. Unlike karst, the perforated landscape here resulted from vigorous erosion by water in weakly cemented sedimentary rock.

Arroyo Tapiado widens after 4.0 miles and sets a straighter course northwest. The canyon divides at 6.3 miles; take the right fork, following the sign indicating "Arroyo Diablo." At 6.7 miles, the road goes up the slope to the right and meanders southeast to join Arroyo Seco del Diablo at 9.0 miles.

Shallow at first, Arroyo Diablo deepens steadily between golden-colored walls of sandstone—quite unlike the gray-green claystone walls you saw in Arroyo Tapiado.

Sandstone concretions, most shaped like balls or bullets, lie half-imbedded in the water-polished walls. Others have completely weathered out and lie on the ground. Between 11.0 and 13.0 miles, there are many interesting tributaries of Arroyo Seco del Diablo to explore via side hikes if you have time. At 12.3 miles, a tributary on the west side leaves the trail and divides into a maze of narrow slot canyons chock-full of concretions, each one a unique sculpture.

Down near the mouth of Arroyo Diablo are some mesquite groves, and a small seep in the floor of the canyon. When you emerge

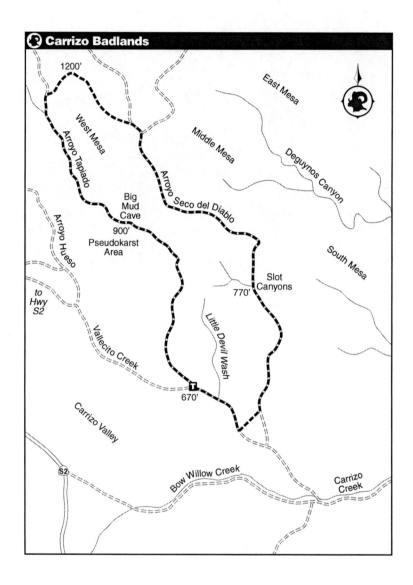

onto flat land just beyond the canyon mouth, save some time and distance by leaving the wheel tracks and turning west and hiking or running cross-country to join the sandy road in Vallecito Creek wash. You'll then turn right to return to your car at the junction of Vallecito Wash and Arroyo Tapiado.

The nearest reliable source of water is Agua Caliente County Park, 4 miles northwest on Highway S-2 from the Palm Spring/Vallecito Wash turnoff.

**Trail Notes**

The caveat about heat and lack of water in this part of the desert can't be overemphasized. December through February is the best time to visit.

**Nature Notes**

Avoid the weekends—especially the holiday weekends—if you don't like sharing these desert washes with too many motor vehicles.

As an alternative to running the entire route, consider employing one mountain bike for every two runners in your group. By taking turns biking and running, you never get tired of either type of exercise.

# RECOMMENDED READING

## BOOKS

Barrios, Dagny. *Runner's World Complete Guide to Trail Running.* Emmaus, PA: Rodale Press, 2003.

Chase, Adam W., and Hobbs, Nancy. *The Ultimate Guide to Trail Running: Everything You Need to Know About Equipment, Finding Trails, Nutrition, Hill Strategy, Racing, Training, Weather, First Aid, and Much More.* The Lyons Press, 2001

Hewitt, Lonnie Burstein, and Moore, Barbara Coffin. *Walking San Diego: Where to Go to Get Away from It All.* 2nd ed. Seattle, WA: Mountaineers Books, 2000.

Jamison, Neal. *Running Through the Wall: Personal Encounters With the Ultramarathon.* Halcottsville, NY: Breakaway Books, 2003.

Lindsay, Lowell, and Lindsay, Diana. *The Anza-Borrego Desert Region: A Guide to the State Park and Adjacent Areas of the Western Colorado Desert.* 4th ed. Berkeley, CA: Wilderness Press, 1998.

Nabakov, Peter. *Indian Running.* Santa Barbara, CA; Capra Press, 1981.

Poulin, Kirsten; Swartz, Stan; and Flaxel, Christina. *Trail Running: From Novice to Master.* Seattle, WA: Mountaineers Books, 2002.

Schad, Jerry. *Afoot and Afield in San Diego County.* 3rd ed. Berkeley, CA: Wilderness Press, 1998.

Schad, Jerry. *Adventure Running.* South Bend, IN: Icarus Press, 1983.

Swartz, Stan; Wolff, Jim; and Shahin, Samir. *50 Trail Runs in Southern California.* Seattle, WA: Mountaineers Books, 2000.

## PERIODICALS

At outdoor, fitness and running-shoe retail outlets around San Diego you can obtain free copies of publications such as *Raceplace San Diego* and *Competitor* magazine. In addition, there are two nationally distributed magazines dealing with trail running: *Trail Runner* and *Ultrarunning*.

## WEBSITES

*Trail Runner* magazine's website includes a page titled "Trail Running San Diego." The page includes contact information for local trail races, running clubs, and running stores:
**www.trailrunnermag.com/features/urban/sandiego.html**

---

**Tell us what you really think** Something unclear, outdated, or just plain wrong in this book? Have a good suggestion for making it better? We welcome reader feedback on all our publications. If we use your suggestion, we'll send you a free book. Please email comments to: update@wildernesspress.com

# INDEX

# ABOUT THE AUTHOR

Photo by Edna Loeb

Jerry Schad's several parallel careers have encompassed interests ranging from astronomy and teaching to photography and writing. He holds a B.A. in astronomy from U.C. Berkeley, an M.S. in astronomy from San Diego State University, and currently chairs the Physical Sciences Department at San Diego Mesa College.

Schad is author of the Afoot and Afield series of Wilderness Press hiking guidebooks for Southern California, and other books on running and bicycling. *Trail Runner's Guide San Diego,* Schad's 13th book, encapsulates his love for running in outdoor locales, a pursuit he took up soon after moving to San Diego in 1972.

Schad has run or hiked many thousands of miles of distinct trails throughout California, in the Southwest, and in Mexico. He is a sub-24-hour finisher of Northern California's 100-mile Western States Endurance Run, and has served in a leadership capacity for outdoor excursions as close as San Diego County and as far away as Madagascar. More information can be found at Schad's website, www.skyphoto.com.

LaVergne, TN USA
17 May 2010
183006LV00003B/185/P